Studies in International Affairs Number 16

THE WEARY AND THE WARY: U.S. AND JAPANESE SECURITY POLICIES IN TRANSITION

by Robert E. Osgood

The Washington Center of Foreign Policy Research
School of Advanced International Studies
The Johns Hopkins University

The Johns Hopkins University Press
Baltimore and London

The Johns Hopkins University Press, Baltimore,
  Maryland 21218
The Johns Hopkins University Press Ltd., London

Library of Congress Catalog Card Number 71-186510
ISBN 0-8018-1393-X (clothbound edition)
ISBN 0-8018-1398-O (paperbound edition)

Originally published, 1972
Paperbound edition, 1972

Library of Congress Cataloging in Publication data
will be found on the last printed page of this book.

FOREWORD

This essay is part of the Washington Center's continuing effort to interpret and reinterpret the salient issues of American foreign policy. Like other books in the Center's Studies in International Affairs series, it aims to illuminate a strand in the larger tapestry of American policy, which we re-examine approximately every four years in *America and the World* (first volume published in 1970).

Changes in the international and domestic environment of policy, accentuated if not created by the reaction to American involvement in the Vietnam war, raise fundamental questions about the direction American policy is taking. Is it toward disengagement, the transfer of power and responsibilities to new centers of power, or merely continued engagement at a lower level of effort and involvement? Or do any such models really apply? The way United States relations with Japan develop in the next decade will go far to determine and register the answer. This essay, which is in part a sequel to Osgood, Packard, and Badgley, *Japan and the United States in Asia* (1968), examines the nature of the changing international environment and the Nixon Doctrine on U.S.-Japanese relations in Asia.

CONTENTS

THE WEARY AND THE WARY

Studies in International Affairs Number 16

I. INTRODUCTION

The United States has reached the end of an era of expanding commitments and involvements in international politics and has begun to retrench. Japan is rapidly attaining the economic dimensions of a superpower,[1] but it rejects the expansion of its military role beyond defense of the homeland and Okinawa. The hesitant positions of these giant states—the one weary, the other wary, of exercising power—provide the setting for a crucial revision of U.S.-Japanese relations over the next decade.

The prospect of America's disengagement from the Far East threatens the security foundation of Japan's postwar foreign policy. It threatens to bring to the forefront of Japanese attention painful and divisive issues that were suppressed when the nation was more confident of American protection—issues concerning the scope of Japan's security interests and military role beyond the homeland. The way Japan and the United States respond to

[1] Japan attained the third highest GNP in 1969. In 1971 the GNP growth rate declined to less than 5 percent, but even if it were to decline permanently to only half the officially projected rate of over 10 percent, it would probably approach, if not surpass, the Soviet GNP before the end of this century. Japan's per capita income ranks only about fifteenth, but it is rising more rapidly than the GNP and can be expected to equal the Soviet per capita income before the end of the 1970s. As the Japanese increasingly recognize, however, these growth indicators do not reflect severe problems of inadequate social infrastructure, excessive pollution, and underdevelopment of service and distribution sectors of the economy.

1

this new situation will determine the future pattern of U.S.-Japanese relations and shape the pattern of international politics in Asia for a generation.

The signing of the treaty for the reversion of Okinawa to Japan foreshadows a basic revision of U.S.-Japanese relations but does not indicate the nature of this revision. The question is whether the revision will take the form of a fundamental redistribution of power in Asia from the United States to Japan or only of new terms of collaboration within the present distribution. The first kind of revision would amount to a major structural change in the pattern of international politics. The latter might move U.S.-Japanese relations in the direction of U.S.-West German relations, qualifying American military preponderance with enhanced Japanese participation in mutual defense. The first kind of revision would entail removal of the constitutional and political restrictions on Japan's military role. The latter would not. But in either case the familiar American tutelage will come to an end.

II. PRINCIPAL TRENDS IN AMERICA'S ASIAN POLICY

The revision of U.S.-Japanese relations will depend greatly on the nature and extent of the revision of America's position in Asia. About the future of American foreign policy, the Japanese are among the most intense and anxious prognosticators but so far they have only fragmentary evidence to go on. If one may judge from the pronouncements and actions of the Nixon administration, and take them at face value for the time being, American policy will be shaped by the following general trends:

a) Firm adherence to the Security Treaty with Japan and to American military commitments in the area.

President Nixon has announced that "in contemplating new commitments we will apply rigorous yardsticks," but a number of statements reaffirm existing commitments; for example, "We will respect the commitments we inherited—both because of their intrinsic merit, and because of the impact of sudden shifts on regional or world stability." [2]

b) A reduced American military presence in Japan and the surrounding area.

The reduction of American airpower and military personnel in Japan, down to minimal levels needed to maintain remaining bases and conduct intelligence gathering (totaling about 30,000 personnel

[2] Richard M. Nixon, *U.S. Foreign Policy for the 1970's,* Report to Congress by the President of the United States, February 25, 1971.

in 1971); the further withdrawal of troops from Okinawa that will accompany reversion; and the withdrawal of 20,000 U.S. military personnel from South Korea, as well as withdrawals from Taiwan and the Philippines, show a distinct trend toward the virtual removal of American ground forces in Northeast Asia during the 1970s, except perhaps for skeleton forces in Japan and South Korea.

c) Somewhat reduced capabilities to intervene with general purpose forces against communist aggression in the area.

Overall reduction of defense expenditures (in "constant dollars," to allow for inflation and salary increases), investment in new strategic weapons systems, and soaring manpower costs, which are more than 60 percent of annual defense expenditures, are leading to the reduction of general purpose forces to below 1964 levels before the start of the Vietnam buildup. The reductions in U.S. ground combat forces, which were made almost entirely in Asia, is not fully compensated for by greater reliance on the mobilization of reserves or projected increases in military assistance (assuming that Congress will permit them). The deactivation of two divisions returning from Vietnam and one returning from Korea will leave about four divisions available for Asian contingencies. Moreover, Secretary of Defense Laird's annual Defense Report for 1971, in describing plans for the 1972–76 defense program, stated: "With regard to U.S. force capabilities in Asia, we do not plan for the long term to maintain separate large U.S. ground combat forces specifically oriented just to this theater, but we do intend to maintain strong air, naval, and support capabilities. . . . In the future, we expect the emphasis in Asia more and more to be placed on U.S. support to our allies who themselves provide the required manpower." [3]

d) A diminished willingness to engage American troops in local conflicts, especially when communist aggression is by a nonnuclear state and largely internal.

One effect of the Vietnam war has been to drive home the lesson that military threats short of unambiguous, direct attacks against an ally must hereafter be dealt with primarily by indigenous forces. Thus the president's second annual report to Congress, although affirming the United States' special obligation to "provide a shield if a nuclear power threatens the freedom of a nation allied with us or of a nation whose survival we consider vital to our security," states that "in cases involving other types of aggression we shall furnish military and economic assistance when requested in accordance with our treaty commitments. But we shall look to the nation directly threatened to assume the primary responsibility of providing the manpower for its defense." [4] The first Report, intended more directly to distinguish Nixon's poli-

---

[3] *Defense Report on President Nixon's Strategy for Peace,* Statement of Secretary of Defense Melvin R. Laird before the U.S. House of Representatives Armed Services Committee, March 9, 1971, p. 77.

[4] Nixon, *U.S. Foreign Policy for the 1970's,* February 25, 1971, pp. 13, 14.

cies from those of his two predecessors, specifically renounced the expectation that U.S. military force would cope with the entire spectrum of threats to allies, particularly when such threats take the form of subversion, guerrilla warfare, or "wars of national liberation": "We may be able to supplement local efforts with economic and military assistance. However, a direct combat role for U.S. general purpose forces arises primarily when insurgency has shaded into external aggression or when there is an overt conventional attack. In such cases, we shall weigh our interests and our commitments, and we shall consider the efforts of our allies, in determining our response." [5]

III. THE MEANING OF THE NIXON DOCTRINE

These indications that the United States is assuming a lower posture in Japan and East Asia are interpreted by the Japanese in the context of the general thrust of the Nixon Doctrine toward a more selective involvement of American power in the world and a greater reliance on allies to take care of their own security. They are also viewed in the light of pressure for retrenchment by American congressmen and domestic groups, pressure which the president himself has characterized as "neo-

[5] Nixon, *U.S. Foreign Policy for the 1970's,* February 18, 1970, p. 127.

isolationism." More profoundly, they are viewed uneasily, in some circles, in the context of suspicions that American society and national will may be fundamentally eroding.

In the minds of the Japanese, who have depended so absolutely on American protection for their recovery of great-power status since World War II, even the slightest signs of the revision of America's position in Asia and the world are bound to call into question the credibility and capability of American power to police East Asia. The questioning, however, does not lead to clear conclusions about how Japan should or will respond to the lowering American posture. Rather, at this point, it aggravates a growing uneasiness about issues of Japanese policy that have been largely suppressed in the course of maintaining a political consensus based largely on economic progress under American military protection.

The Japanese, therefore, are rather anxious interpreters of the Nixon Doctrine, inclined to regard official articulations as a textbook for future policies but not sure of their meaning. Thus they wonder about the internal consistency of the Nixon Doctrine. How can it reconcile the maintenance of American commitments with the reduction of American capabilities to support them? Is it really just a rationalization of budgetary stringencies and domestic political constraints? Does it foreshadow the abandonment of Asian security, a greater reliance on tactical nuclear weapons, an effort to shift military burdens to other and unwilling shoulders?

The full meaning of the Nixon Doctrine will presumably unfold as events give life to a set of pronouncements which administration spokesmen have warned us not to regard as a "recipe book," but in the president's annual reports to Congress we already have the benefit of the most comprehensive and systematic formulation of the rationale of American policy that any administration has undertaken. These efforts to outline American foreign policy for the 1970s, together with the administration's first efforts to fill in the outline with action, suggest several possible explanations, not necessarily mutually exclusive, of how the administration proposes to keep power in balance with commitments— one of the classic tests of a solvent policy. Whether they are valid explanations is another question, which can be answered definitely only in retrospect a number of years from now. But in the meantime, if the following assessment is correct, one must grant that the government at least intends the Nixon Doctrine to be more than a thin rationalization of domestically inspired retrenchment. In the White House the doctrine is seen as a calculated strategy of foreign policy integrally related to specific concepts of national interest, national power, and the international environment.

A. *Explanation:* The Nixon Doctrine, although reaffirming American commitments, may also be based on such a downgrading of America's interests that the disposition to support commitments with armed force is substantially diminished. Hence, reduced military capabilities will still be sufficient to support commitments under conditions in which force could be used consistently with America's vital interests as the nation and the government see them.

Assessment: Judging from presidential statements and actions, the American government continues to place a high value on the maintenance of non-communist governments in Asia, including South Vietnam. But anyone who knows the foreign relations bureaucracy knows that the familiar rationale for intervention against communist aggression in the Third World—the prevailing belief in the indivisibility of peace and the interconnectedness of dominoes, based on the application of the interwar lessons to postwar interests—has ceased to carry conviction. Moreover, the reevaluation of American interests is implicit in numerous official statements; for example, statements acknowledging that America's "psychological resources" have been strained by overinvolvement, that the United States must apply more scrupulous criteria of national interest to future commitments, and that the enthusiasm for asserting American power in behalf of the security and independence of others, as expressed in President Kennedy's oft-quoted inaugural address, was excessive and is now outdated, particularly with respect to the Third World.[6] In Asia the government evidently shares the general opinion that American

[6] In his inaugural address on January 20, 1961, President Kennedy said, "Let every nation know, whether it wishes us well or ill, that we shall pay any price, bear any burden, meet any hardship, support any friend, oppose any foe to assure the survival and the success of liberty." Although these oft-quoted words do represent the exuberant spirit of national self-assertion and mission that characterized much of the Kennedy administration, a historian of this period might want to balance them with Kennedy's address at the University of Washington on November 16, 1961, delivered in a chastened mood after the involvements in Laos, the Bay of Pigs, and Berlin: "We must face the fact that the United States is neither omnipotent nor omniscient, that we are only six per cent of the world's population, and we cannot right every wrong or reverse each adversity, and that therefore there cannot be an American solution for every world problem."

interests became inflated far beyond objective security needs simply by the involvement of American power and prestige. For the future, therefore, it affirms that "we are not involved in the world because we have commitments; we have commitments because we are involved. Our interest must shape our commitments, rather than the other way around." [7]

B. *Explanation:* The Nixon administration, like the Eisenhower administration, may base the "sufficiency" of reduced nonnuclear capabilities to support existing commitments on the adoption of a new strategy for using total capabilities more efficiently. Thus President Eisenhower and Secretary of State Dulles, in the period of retrenchment following the Korean war, announced a strategy of greater reliance on nuclear responses to threats of conventional aggression in order to deter or fight future Korean wars at less cost in manpower.

Assessment: Secretary of Defense Laird has hailed a "new national security strategy of realistic deterrence." The administration has announced that the United States will not necessarily "limit its responses to the level or intensity chosen by an enemy." Some parts of the Pentagon show unflagging interest in utilizing modern tactical nuclear weapons to provide more effective firepower. But although these strategic footprints lend credence to the view that the Nixon administration is following the Eisenhower-Dulles path, in reality this administration is as wedded to the strategy of flexible and controlled response as were the Kennedy and John-

---

[7] This statement appeared in the president's first annual *Report* (p. 7) and was quoted in the second (p. 13).

son administrations. Indeed, it has reemphasized the importance of general purpose forces in a period of acknowledged strategic parity with the Soviet Union. For all practical purposes the option of returning to the Eisenhower-Dulles strategy is foreclosed. So much has happened in the last two decades to raise inhibitions against the first use of nuclear weapons— especially in Asia—that President Nixon felt called upon to affirm publicly that the United States would not use nuclear weapons in Vietnam.[8]

C. *Explanation:* The Nixon administration may believe that reduced conventional military capabilities remain adequate because the communist military

---

[8] When South Vietnamese forces moved into Laos in February, 1971, the Chinese press and some American observers expressed concern that the United States would use tactical nuclear weapons in order to avoid defeat. In a press conference on February 17, President Nixon, when asked whether the United States would impose any limits on the use of its airpower in protecting the remaining American forces in South Vietnam, said: "I am not going to place any limitation upon the use of airpower except, of course, to rule out a rather ridiculous suggestion that is made from time to time . . . that our airpower might include the use of tactical nuclear weapons." Evidently referring to a position he had taken privately, the president went on to say, "As you know . . . this has been speculated on for a period of five years and I have said for a period of five years that it is not an area where the use of nuclear weapons, in any form, is either needed or would be wise" (*New York Times,* February 18, 1971, p. 14). This statement was in striking contrast to the position that Vice-President Nixon took when the North Vietnamese were besieging the French garrison at Dien Bien Phu in 1955. On March 17, 1955, Nixon said: "It is foolish to talk about the possibility that the weapons which might be used in the event war breaks out in the Pacific would be limited to the conventional Korean and World War II types of explosives. . . . Tactical atomic explosives are now conventional and will be used against the military targets of any aggressive force."

threat against states with which the United States has military commitments has declined.

Assessment: The administration is not counting on a significant reduction of the Soviet threat in light of the Soviet Union's extension of its naval strength and reach, its worrisome involvement in the Middle East cauldron, and an ominous but uncertain Soviet inclination to push for more than strategic parity or a second-strike deterrent for "assured destruction" requires. In Asia, on the other hand, it is evidently betting heavily on the communist threat being substantially lower than it was commonly estimated to be five or ten years ago, partly because the threat was overestimated and partly because it has declined. Most notable is the official downgrading of the Chinese military threat, principally because of the Sino-Soviet split. The other side of the reduced threat is the presumed decreased vulnerability of Asian states to communist aggression. Thus the president's second annual Report to Congress asserts, "Asia of today is vastly different from the Asia which required, over the past several decades, so activist an American role. Asian nations now generally have a strong and confident sense of their own national identity and future. They have generally established healthier relationships with each other and with the outside world. They have created institutions of proven vitality. Their armed forces are stronger." [9]

D. *Explanation:* The Nixon administration, while downgrading the communist military threat, may also have upgraded its estimate of the capacity of

[9] Nixon, *U.S. Foreign Policy for the 1970's,* February 25, 1971, p. 94.

other states to take care of their own military security.

Assessment: The growing self-reliance of countries—individually, regionally, and in partnership with the United States—is a pervasive theme in the president's annual reports to Congress. The second report stresses a vigorous, active regionalism as one of the new realities of Asia leading to greater confidence and strength in the area. Withdrawals of American forces from Vietnam, South Korea, Taiwan, the Philippines, and Japan indicate a limited transfer of responsibilities for national defense from the United States to allies. But whereas this transfer entails a reduction of American material support, it does not clearly envisage other states' supplanting America's security role. Thus, some groups in the Pentagon notwithstanding, the U.S. government does not expect or desire Japan to assume the security role the United States has played in East Asia. As for regional cooperation, the government evidently does not expect the development of anything more than economic and political cooperation for a long time to come. Partly in recognition of the limits of self-reliance, the president's second report emphasizes that the Nixon Doctrine "should not be thought of primarily as the sharing of burdens or the lightening of our load. . . . In effect, we are encouraging countries to participate in the creation of plans and the designing of programs." [10]

E. *Explanation:* The Nixon Doctrine may be based on the belief that the United States, in the exuberance of reasserting its power and prestige after Sputnik and the Cuban missile crisis, created

[10] Ibid., p. 11.

greater military capabilities for fighting limited wars than either its interests or the threat to them required; so the reduction of capabilities to the levels that existed before the United States intervened in Vietnam with major troop contingents in 1965 amounts to restoring a proper ratio between capabilities and commitments.

Assessment: Administration spokesmen contend that America's general purpose forces and its naval and air units available for Asian contingencies are, after all, still sizable and quite adequate when evaluated country by country (as in South Korea) according to the local needs, rather than by an overall comparison to some level of forces in the past. Thus the administration's abandonment of the never fully implemented $2\frac{1}{2}$-war military planning objective of the previous administration (that is, the objective of being prepared to fight a major war in Europe and Asia and a minor war somewhere else simultaneously) in favor of a $1\frac{1}{2}$-war objective is regarded as an overdue adjustment, stimulated by budgetary and political constraints, to changing conditions in international politics that have been developing over the last decade or so—notably the Sino-Soviet split, the economic and psychological resurgence of Western Europe and Japan, the successful containment of Soviet military expansion, and the growing resistance of new and poor states to communist takeover.

F. *Explanation:* The Nixon administration may count on a more active diplomacy in an increasingly multipolar structure of power to constrain and moderate the external relations of the Soviet Union and China and thereby diminish the need for the direct involvement of American military power and for the maintenance of previous levels of American armed forces.

Assessment: This could be the most important aspect of the framework of international politics within which the administration views the power equation. But it is only adumbrated in official state-views and actions, the full significance of which we shall not be able to comprehend until this transitional period is supplanted by a more stable structure of international relationships. In the president's first annual report to Congress an "era of negotiation" is said to be supplanting an "era of confrontation." More revealing is the president's second annual report, which looks forward to a "new and more stable international structure" in which other states will undertake a larger, more active and independent role while the United States restricts its role. In Asia, America's "restructuring" of its "posture" is expected to "set in train the readjustment of the whole international order in the Pacific region," where the United States has been "the heart of the general equilibrium which has been maintained for the past twenty years." In pursuit of this restruc-turing the United States "will be striving to estab-lish a new and stable structure reflecting the renewed vigor of the smaller Asian states, the expanding role of Japan, and the changing interests of the Soviet Union and the Peoples Republic of China." Since "it is a truism that an international order cannot be secure if one of the major powers remains largely outside it and hostile toward it . . . there will be no more important challenge than that of drawing the Peoples Republic of China into a constructive relationship with the world community, and particularly with the rest of Asia." [11] These words give special meaning to the American visits to Peking. They recall passages in Henry Kissinger's *World Restored* expounding the problems during and after the Congress of Vienna of constructing and maintaining a stable multipolar system of international order that would minimize the resort to force. They presage a period of diplomatic maneuver within the constraints of a multipolar equilibrium, replacing the system of "confrontation" in which the United States carried such a preponderant burden of the responsibilities for international order.

If these assessments provide a fairly accurate picture of how the Nixon administration views American interests, commitments, and capabilities, it indicates that the U.S. government intends to bring about a rather fundamental transformation of America's stance in Asia. This transformation, if its underlying premises are correct, need not, objectively, require a drastic change in Japan's security or in Japan's military role. But this does not mean that Japan will in fact view the transformation of American policy with equanimity. Moreover, the history of the cold war shows how misleading it may be to extrapolate American actions from American intentions, since actions inevitably result from unforeseen external events. For this reason one must note that implementation of the Nixon Doctrine depends critically on fallible assumptions about unpredictable conditions, such as the nature of the communist threat to American interests in Asia. Not the least of these conditions is America's still

[11] Ibid., pp. 97–98, 105–6.

formative view of its basic interests in the outside world. Consequently, Japanese officials and analysts must base their responses to America's changing position in Asia on a set of inferences that are highly contingent. In doing so, they will be acutely conscious of the effect that every sign of a change in Japan's policy in Asia may exert on America's position. They know that uneasy speculation in the United States, as elsewhere, about trends in Japan's policy is almost as intense, if less widespread and articulate, as concern in Japan about the meaning of the Nixon Doctrine.

IV. JAPAN'S INHIBITED MILITARY ROLE

The prospect of a substantial reduction of American effort and involvement in Asia after such a long period of preponderance, no matter how the American government may explain it, inevitably stimulates speculation that Japan may compensate for this reduction with a larger military role of its own. Peking and Moscow profess to see the rise of Japanese militarism as a sure result of the Nixon Doctrine and the Japanese search for resources and markets in Southeast Asia. Southeast Asians, with bitter memories of Japan's Greater East Asia Co-Prosperity Sphere, see the Nixon Doctrine in conjunction with growing Japanese-Chinese economic and political competition leading to the projection of Japanese military power in the area.

Expectations of Japan's ascendance as a military power, however, would exist even if one assumed no waning of confidence in American protection. Simply from the standpoint of the traditional conduct of great powers in history, one might expect Japan to throw its military weight on Asian scales as it rapidly reaches the magnitude of an economic superpower, expands its economic and political interests, and seeks to assert its autonomy in self-defense and foreign policy generally. This development seems all the more likely because Asia is hardly a placid, stable environment. Rather, it is an area where the interests of two major states basically hostile to Japan (The People's Republic of China and the Soviet Union) converge, where a number of states are subject to foreign penetration, and where several local national conflicts could result in war.

But to rest the question of Japan's future role in Asia on these generalities would be much too simple. One must also take into account general characteristics of the international system and specific characteristics of Japan's external relations that exert a different tendency.

Among the general characteristics of the international system is the historically novel disparity of military power—in magnitude, function, and geographical reach—between the two first-rank states and their allies, the once great, now second-rank states. This disparity tends to reduce the incentive, as well as the relative capacity, of the second-rank states to play the balance-of-power game on the central stage of international politics as long as they can count on a superpower to play the game in their behalf. Furthermore, having gone through their period of expanding interests and power some decades ago and having been chastened by the experience of two world wars, the second-rank states have long since accommodated themselves to retrenchment of their foreign interests and involvements. And their retrenchment is now accentuated by domestic preoccupations. In this respect, the failure of de Gaulle's France to achieve far-reaching diplomatic goals with the lever of an autonomous military policy has been sobering. For these states, therefore, the utility of military power beyond self-defense may be limited to the support of status. They can pursue the more tangible and specific stakes of international politics, such as foreign trade and investment, without projecting military power beyond their borders. Moreover, to some extent their military *potential* gives weight to their external political influence without the liabilities of maintaining and deploying real forces-in-being.

In Japan these systemic factors limiting its military/political role are greatly reinforced by special inhibitions derived from the trauma of defeat and nuclear destruction in World War II. These inhibitions are codified in the war-renouncing clause, Article 9 of the postwar Japanese Constitution, which is interpreted as confining Japanese military functions to "self-defense" and prohibiting "offensive" weapons.[12] They are given political reality by

---

[12] Article 9 provides that "the Japanese people forever renounce war as a sovereign right of the nation and the threat or use of force as a means of settling international disputes.

"In order to accomplish the aim of the preceding paragraph, land, sea, and air forces, as well as other war potential, will

the massive domestic consensus against stretching or amending the Constitution to permit a larger role than insular defense. Within the dominant government party, the Liberal Democratic party (LDP), few support a broader interpretation of self-defense even within the right-wing faction. All the opposition parties, including those who have supported the gradual increase of the Self-Defense Forces in recent years, oppose a broader military role.

Domestic inhibitions against a larger military role spring partly from opposition to a resurgence of "militarism" and partly from satisfaction with the practical advantages of avoiding large defense burdens; but more importantly they spring from the fear of provoking and frightening other nations with whom Japan is eager to have good relations. Painfully conscious of the legacy of foreign suspicion and antipathy stemming from Japanese expansion in the 1930s and during World War II, the Japanese are intent upon gaining the good opinion of others and,

---

never be maintained. . . ." The Japanese Supreme Court in December, 1959, upheld the prevailing view that this article does not deny the inherent right of self-defense and preparation for self-defense against armed attack. However, it has been interpreted to prohibit overseas dispatch of forces and the possession of weapons that might take offensive action against other states, such as long-range bombers, offensive aircraft carriers, and long-range missiles. Nuclear weapons are also generally considered to be prohibited by Article 9, but officially the legal obstacle to nuclear weapons production lies in Article 2 of Japan's Atomic Energy Act and in the government's adoption of the three nonnuclear principles of not manufacturing, possessing, or bringing nuclear weapons into Japan. The government has said that "small" or "tactical" nuclear weapons designed for self-defense only would not violate the Constitution, but it has renounced acquisition of such weapons as a matter of policy. See the so-called Defense White Paper, "Japan's Defense," issued by the Japanese Defense Agency in October, 1970.

incidentally, reaping the advantages of a growing trade with them, by showing irrefutably that Japan is now a peaceful, nonmilitaristic nation despite its great economic power.

Their determination to confine Japan's military role to the defense of the homeland is undergirded by the conviction that Japan's geographical insularity makes it virtually invulnerable to foreign aggression, at least as long as it preserves internal order and maintains its alliance with the United States. In this connection the Japanese point out to American visitors that their salient historical memories pertain only to Japan expanding from the homeland to the mainland or Taiwan, not to the homeland being invaded or threatened by others. All the more reason, they explain, that they should associate power politics with an aggressive and militaristic policy—which, it is felt, Japan must now thoroughly repudiate—and not with the legitimate imperatives of security, which are confined to self-defense.

Indeed, Americans discussing the basic premises of foreign and military policy with Japanese are bound to be struck by the difference of outlook between the Japanese view of security and what has been the prevailing American approach, although this difference is less marked when the Japanese view is compared to that of young Americans who have no historical memories of the interwar period or the origins of the cold war. It is sobering to remember, however, that only a few decades ago, before World War II, Americans too conceived of their security interests almost entirely in terms of protecting the homeland from invasion. It is only since World

War II that American policymakers, moved by the lessons of the interwar period and the experience of containing Soviet expansion, have taken it for granted that American security depends, centrally, upon discouraging or stopping communist armed aggression even against remote states whose independence is intrinsically unimportant to American security. The rapid transformation of the American view of national security from an insular to a global outlook shows the limits of geography and tradition in determining foreign policy. It shows that the premises of foreign and military policy can be profoundly, and even quickly, altered by basic structural changes in the configurations of national power and interests within which a powerful state is compelled to pursue its vital interests.

The Japanese, however, do not foresee any such structural changes. They are aware of the mutable international conditions—including assured American protection—under which Japan has been able to regain its national self-confidence, generate an economic miracle, and maintain remarkable political stability. But they are not in a mood to abandon self-denying policies that have worked so well unless and until drastic changes in Japan's international environment unmistakably impinge upon tangible interests essential to national prosperity and defense.

For these reasons there is widespread agreement inside and outside the government that although Japan has become a powerful "economic animal," it must not and need not become a commensurate military power. This conjunction of economic virility and military impotence presupposes a historical anomaly, which might quickly give way if the domestic or

international political environment were to change
drastically. But the Japanese are determined to make
the anomaly stick, and they insist that it is firmly
rooted in a national consensus of great stability.
They are convinced that Japan, for the indefinite
future, is launched on the novel historical experiment
of becoming the first nonmilitary superpower.[13]

V. JAPAN'S CONCEPTION OF EXTERNAL INTERESTS

The foregoing discussion suggests that Japan's
foreign and military policy, in its major outlines, is
quite stable, but that its stability is based on some
basic features of the international environment that
are subject to change.

Of course, domestic changes might also affect
Japan's foreign and military policy. However, the
pattern of voting that has enabled the Liberal

[13] Actually, Japanese, unlike Herman Kahn and some other
western observers, do not refer to Japan as a superpower but
only as an "economic giant" (or, in a slightly derogatory vein,
"economic animal"). However, they do think of Japan as a
rising power in the "second-rank" or "middle-weight" class of
France, West Germany, the United Kingdom, and China.
Former Defense Minister Nakasone described Japan's conception of its rank in the following words: "We have undertaken an unprecedented experiment to remain a militarily
medium, nonnuclear nation—potentially influential through our
economic-industrial potential but militarily strong enough only
to defend herself if attacked" (speech delivered at Foreign
Correspondents' Club of Japan, Tokyo, December 1, 1970).

Democratic party to remain dominant for over twenty years seems remarkably stable, representing a consensus based on the primacy of domestic economic goals. Equally stable is the prewar "establishment" of politicians, bureaucrats, and businessmen who run the country's internal and external affairs. The "old guard" is aging and its rural base of support is shrinking, but the opposition is fragmented. Barring a serious economic dislocation, important changes in the domestic political balance seem less likely to be the independent cause of basic policy changes than to result from the impact of changes in the international environment on foreign and defense policy.

It would be fruitless to try to predict the Asian international environment for more than a few years ahead, but it is important to recognize the principal features of the environment that now underlie and could in the future change Japan's outlook, perhaps very quickly. These features will be apparent in the following examination of four major determinants of Japan's present outlook: (1) Japan's conception of its external interests, (2) its perception of the threats to these interests, (3) its view of America's security role, and (4) the attitude of other states toward Japanese power. We will examine the first determinant in this section.

Japan's military policies, like those of the United States and other nations, are affected by the scope and value of those external interests that seem to require military support. The correlation between interests and military policies is not complete because military policies are affected not only by many domestic conditions but also by the interplay of other international conditions. Nonetheless, foreign interests are the most fundamental determinant of a nation's military policies. In Japan's case they may provide an early clue to possible changes in military policy, because internal and external conditions are conspiring to make the Japanese more conscious of latent security interests in the surrounding environment, and because Japan's commercial and diplomatic interests are rapidly expanding.

Until recently the Japanese have had little incentive to consider overseas interests in terms of military power, and particularly not in terms of their own power. They were content to leave to the United States the arduous and, in their eyes, slightly disreputable task of managing a balance of power. Under American tutelage they were moved by the psychology of a dependent state renouncing power politics. Their foreign interests and policies beyond consolidating American protection were inchoate and subordinate to those of their protector. But now the restoration of Japanese self-confidence and national pride; Japanese consciousness of having become an economic giant; the striking development of Japanese trade and commerce in Southeast Asia and all over the world; and the prospect of American retrenchment in Asia have begun to make the Japanese aware of independent overseas interests which the United States may not guarantee. Indeed, some of the most important policy concerns of Japan pertain to issues on which American policies may differ (as in relations with Peking) and American interests may diverge (as in trade).

The development and crystallization of independent Japanese foreign interests do not necessarily lead to an overseas Japanese military policy, but it is worth noting that this is the beginning of a process that has led great powers in the past to project their military power beyond their boundaries—not necessarily for acquisitive ends but simply for security. To understand this phenomenon one must appreciate the flexibility of the concept of national security.

Arnold Wolfers perceptively described the protean quality of the concept in one of his classic essays, "National Security as an Ambiguous Symbol," published in 1952.[14] "Security," he observed, "commonly includes more than the 'core value' of national independence and territorial integrity." It "covers a range of goals so wide that highly divergent policies can be interpreted as policies of security." Since security is the absence of a threat or the feeling of a threat to national values, "efforts for security by a particular nation will tend to vary, other things being equal, with the range of values for which protection is being sought." And these values typically include "rank, respect, material possessions, and special privileges." They include what Wolfers in another essay called "milieu goals"; that is, favorable conditions in the international environment, including balances of power and spheres of influence, which nations seek in order to protect more immediate values, and which then become new national values requiring protection themselves. Although national security does not depend on the power of coercion alone, military power has always been an indispensable ingredient of national security for states with important external interests which they

[14] Reprinted in his *Discord and Collaboration* (Baltimore: Johns Hopkins Press, 1962), chap. 10.

are not willing to entrust to an ally or to the vicissitudes of countervailing power managed by others.

If Japan were to follow this historic path in the pursuit of national security, one would expect its overseas military policy to begin with the protection of interests closest to the homeland and then to expand to cover more remote interests and milieu goals. So far, few Japanese believe that Japan should try to support external interests with its own armed forces, and the deployment of Japanese troops abroad is now virtually unthinkable. Nonetheless, the Japanese government and many Japanese outside the government are conscious of national interests beyond the defense of the homeland which are regarded as security interests. Among these interests the independence of South Korea and, to a lesser extent, Taiwan are most prominent. Thus when Prime Minister Sato affirmed, in the official communique at the close of the Nixon-Sato conference of November, 1969, that the security of South Korea is "essential" to Japan's security, and that Taiwan is "a most important factor for the security of Japan," he was expressing a not uncommon view of Japan's security interests, although he overstated the magnitude of these interests in deference to the expediencies of gaining U.S. senatorial approval of Okinawan reversion.

This feeling that the security of South Korea and Taiwan is important to the security of Japan transcends an objectively provable relationship between the fate of these countries and Japan's core values. It is based on a conventional geopolitical outlook, a latent fear of mainland China's ambitions in the area, and the fact that Japan conducts over 6 percent of its trade with these countries,[15] who, in turn, trade from 40 to 45 percent of their combined imports and exports with Japan. But underlying these factors there are more obscure feelings of interdependence stemming from historical memories of Japan's occupation of these two countries and perhaps from deeper conceptions of national interest that have nothing to do with security. Some Japanese who share the general consensus on foreign policy, including government officials, contend that this view of Japanese security interests is unwarranted by a coldly objective assessment of the facts, as opposed to suppositions based on outmoded geopolitical notions and subjective intuitions. Nevertheless, it seems safe to bet that the confirmed retrenchment by the United States, if coupled by sustained Chinese hostility toward Japan, would make Japan as a whole quite conscious of special security interests in its Asian backyard.

Some Japanese respond to a more abstract interest in the security of the sea-lanes. Although they do not think of this interest in terms of threat scenarios and specific contingencies, they are conscious of Japan's economic dependence on the security of these lifelines, and they recall the U.S. oil embargo that compelled Japan to choose between war with the United States or economic strangulation.

Beyond the Korean peninsula and the Straits of Taiwan, Japanese interests seem less clearly related to perceptions of national security, but they are

[15] Japan's trade with Taiwan is 2 to 2½ percent of its world trade; with South Korea, 4 percent. Trade with Hong Kong is almost as great as with Taiwan, which in turn is almost as large as with mainland China.

moving in this direction. Thus the Japanese are rapidly becoming more conscious of important economic interests in Southeast Asia (Burma, Cambodia, Laos, Indochina, Thailand, Malaysia, Singapore, Philippines, and Indonesia) and of the dependence of these interests on the security and stability of the area. The area comprises about 12 percent of Japan's total trade, ranking just behind Europe and North America, and this proportion may grow. Its agricultural and mineral resources (including Indonesian oil) make it critical to Japan's industrial economy. Heavy Japanese investments will reinforce Japan's ties to the area. No less critical to Japan's economic welfare is unimpeded passage through the Strait of Malacca, through which pass almost all of Japan's rising petroleum imports, which now account for over 75 percent of Japan's energy consumption as opposed to 25 percent in 1965.[16]

The importance of Southeast Asia to Japan was recognized in Japan's sponsorship in 1966 of an annual Ministerial Conference on Southeast Asian Economic Development and, since then, in official statements that Japan will devote the bulk of its foreign aid programs (which the government has pledged to make 1 percent of Japan's annual GNP by 1975) to the area. There can be no doubt that such measures of economic cooperation manifest a basic political interest in the internal stability, peace,

[16] If the Strait of Malacca were closed, Japanese ships going to and from the Middle East could use the strait of Lombok. But, even with the greater depth of Lombok now, which permits larger tankers to pass through, Malacca is significantly cheaper because of the shorter travel distance it affords.

and friendship of the area. This political interest, moreover, is not rooted entirely in economic considerations. Memories of Japan's prewar Greater East Asia Co-Prosperity Sphere—memories in which shame and disappointment are qualified by pride and a sense of missed opportunities—mingle with more recent political concerns about the destabilizing effects of economic backwardness upon the international environment.

Nonetheless, Japan's rising consciousness of important economic and political interests in Southeast Asia falls short of making the area more than a *latent* security interest in Japanese eyes. Geographical remoteness and the absence of a discernible Chinese military threat make Southeast Asia seem like a safe area of economic expansion free from military implications for Japan for the time being.

In speculating about the sources of Japanese defense policies, however, one must also bear in mind that many states now, as always in history, want to project military power abroad for reasons only tangentially related to material welfare and security. They want such things as status and diplomatic weight, and they want to be able to support their interests in territorial and other disputes.

In recent years high Japanese officials have openly exhorted the nation to elevate its international status and get rid of its "negative pacifism" and its "nuclear allergy." Consistent with this effort to restore national pride, Japan has claimed and gained membership in the Conference of the Committee on Disarmament (formerly Eighteen-Nation Disarmament Committee) and asserted its desire to become a permanent member of the United Nations Security

Council. On the other hand, it is precisely in the realm of asserting national pride and will that domestic and foreign opposition to Japanese military policy is strongest. Indeed, the restoration of Japan's international status is commonly believed to depend on renouncing any military role beyond insular defense. Only with respect to acquiring nuclear weapons have a few Japanese suggested that status is now a reason for a larger military role; and even then self-defense, not status, is the principal argument. Chinese nuclear bragging and blackmail or the creation of an Indian or Israeli nuclear force might reveal a more widespread sentiment for nuclear status than one would suspect from current evidence. But from present indications one must conclude that if status becomes a motive for a larger military policy, it will only be as an increment to compelling security motives.

The same generalization can be made about the pursuit of a larger military role for the sake of diplomatic weight or the support of national interests in territorial and other disputes, unless Japan's surrounding international environment were to become far more inhospitable than one can foresee. To undergird the diplomatic objectives that Japan is likely to pursue in the next decade, the nation's vast economic strength and military potential will probably provide enough weight to satisfy all but a few chauvinists who would seek a larger military role for other reasons in any event. On the other hand, two territorial disputes might at least contribute to the expansion of Japan's naval and air role.

One territorial dispute concerns Japan's claim to the uninhabited islands of Senkaku in the China Sea.

The value of these islands lies in the great estimated oil resources on the continental shelf in the area north toward Japan and Korea, where extensive drilling is planned. Currently under U.S. administration as a part of the Ryukyus, the Senkaku will revert to Japan in 1972. But both the communist Chinese and the Nationalist Chinese claim jurisdiction on the same basis of geological, geographical, and historical arguments. For the Republic of China the islands are an issue of national pride, although the government is quietly working on a *modus vivendi* with Japan. The People's Republic of China exploits the issue as a basis for charges against Japanese "militarism" on the one hand and Nationalist softness in the face of Japanese imperialism on the other. Japan tries to keep the issue quiet. The United States hopes to dissociate itself from the controversy. The issue per se is unlikely to affect Japanese military policy. But if (for whatever reasons) Japan should be inclined to expand its navy, the Senkaku would provide an argument more persuasive and politically acceptable than either the abstract objective of protecting sea-lanes or the explicit objective of countering Soviet naval power.

Another possible stimulant to Japanese military concerns in neighboring waters is Japan's desire to reclaim ownership of certain islands north of Hokkaido in the Kuriles chain which the Soviet Union has occupied since 1945. Japanese spokesmen single out the four southernmost islands and, recently, particularly the two islands closest to Hokkaido (Habomai and Shikotan) as candidates for reversion.[17] But not even in Hokkaido does Japanese

[17] In 1956 Japan prepared to renounce claims to southern

sentiment for reversion approach the intensity of sentiment for Okinawan reversion. In the latter case public opinion impelled the government to act; in the former it is principally the government that generates claims of sovereignty. The islands are uninhabited. No fighting took place on them in World War II. Their importance to Japan, apart from fishing in the area, is not their intrinsic value but their value as stakes of national pride and as bargaining counters. From the Soviet standpoint their military value as outposts in the Sea of Okhotsk is minimal. But so far, although Soviet leaders have occasionally implied that these islands might revert to Japan in return for Japanese favors,[18] Moscow has regarded the cost of giving them up, in light of the precedent of returning wartime treaty acquisitions, as outweighing anything it could gain in its relations with Japan. Continued Soviet intransigence on reversion might conceivably be used as an argument in Japan for naval increases, but it is scarcely credible that Japan would contemplate military threats or encounters over the Northern Islands for any purpose.

Sakhalin and the northern Kuriles in return for the reversion of Kunahsin, Etorofu, Habomai, and Shikotan. The Soviets refused and offered instead to return the latter two if Japan renounced its claims to the rest. Japan refused.

[18] In 1960 the Soviets told Japan that Habomai and Shikotan could only be returned when all the foreign troops had left Japan and a treaty with the Soviet Union had been signed. In 1964 Khrushchev told a Diet delegation that "if the Americans will give back Okinawa, feel free to take these islands from us. We will be cabling Tokyo on the day Okinawa returns to Japan." Quoted in Ishimoto, "The Northern Territories and a Peace Treaty with the USSR," *Annual Review of the Japan Institute of International Affairs,* 4 (1965–68) : 46.

VI. PERCEIVED THREATS TO JAPANESE INTERESTS

The Japanese approach to military policies is marked by the absence of any but the most hypothetical perception of an armed threat to the homeland or to vital foreign interests. In Japanese eyes the only states that might conceivably threaten the homeland are the People's Republic of China and the Soviet Union. These two states and North Korea pose the only potential threats to overseas interests that Japan might wish to counter with its own military power under some hypothetical conditions.

Polls confirm the common observation of visitors and the Japanese themselves that the Japanese have a deep distrust of the Russians, going back at least as far as the Russo-Japanese War, and that they expect the worst from them as a general rule. High-handed Soviet conduct with respect to the Northern Islands and Japanese fishing have kept this antipathy alive. Toward the Chinese they are more ambivalent, admiring their culture and feeling a certain racial affinity but entertaining a rather unspecific feeling of being threatened by a hostile regime, especially when Peking accentuates its verbal campaign against Japanese "militarism." Neither communist state, however, is believed to have any intention of attacking or threatening to attack the homeland. And the Chinese do not have the capability. To take either threat seriously the Japanese would have to fear the coincidence of an internal upheaval and the withdrawal of the American nuclear umbrella.

As for threats to external interests, another North

Korean move to unify the peninsula under communist rule is the most important and likely threat in
Japanese eyes, although the threat is regarded as
quite low as long as there are American forces in
South Korea. A Chinese attack on Taiwan is considered even less likely, but some officials and outside
analysts regard it as a contingency worth taking into
account in the long run if the United States were to
abandon its protection of the island.

In Southeast Asia the relatively few Japanese
who think about the area in such terms see Peking
looking for easy opportunities to extend Chinese
influence, including opportunities to support revolutionary and subversive forces. But their estimate of
Chinese capability to intervene militarily in the area
is so low and the prospect of Japan countering any
such intervention seems so unrealistic at this time
that the hypothetical threat does not really enter
into Japanese thinking. Similarly with the Strait of
Malacca or the Indian Ocean, the few Japanese who
are conscious of the importance to the Japanese
economy of the sea route to the Middle East do not
see any real possibility of a communist threat to cut
off this lifeline. The unreal quality of the contingency
is perhaps enhanced by the view that it is politically
out of the question for Japan to consider protecting
the sea-lanes anyway.

Despite the low estimate of a Chinese military
threat to Japan's foreign interests, the prospect of
communist China becoming an active nuclear power
vaguely frightens many Japanese.[19] The prospect is

[19] Two annual national opinion polls conducted by the news-
paper *Mainichi* in 1969 and 1970 produced the following

already sufficiently worrisome to have stimulated a minor public debate in Japan about Japan's nuclear option. Private negotiations and public discussions preceding Japan's signing of the Non-Proliferation Treaty sharpened the debate. A few Japanese officials, politicians, and intellectuals have reached the conclusion that China's nuclear program, together with the declining credibility of America's nuclear umbrella, pose a potentially serious threat to the peace and security of Japan's international environment. Before the end of the 1970s, they reason, China will have a nuclear force that can hold Asian states hostage and perhaps even threaten to strike the United States directly if it should dare come to the defense of the hostages. This will tend to neutralize the deterrent effect of American nuclear weapons in Asia and induce the Chinese to be more adventurous in applying pressure—not excluding military pressure—against the nonnuclear states along its periphery.

Only a handful of those few Japanese who articulate the potential Chinese nuclear threat, however, conclude openly that Japan must therefore have its own nuclear weapons. Moreover, the great majority of officials and analysts concerned with defense issues deny that China's nuclear program will seriously affect Japan's vital foreign interests. Former Defense Minister Nakasone, for instance, enlarging

---

answers (in percent) to evaluations of "nuclear armament of Communist China":

Answer	April, 1969	March, 1970
Very dreadful	43	46
A little dreadful	35	32
Not too dreadful	15	14
Not dreadful at all	3	3

upon an official theme that Japan is protected by the stabilizing influence of the superpower balance (which he called "environmental deterrence"), contended that when China acquires long-range nuclear missiles the bipolar U.S.-Soviet deadlock will simply become tripolar, so that Japanese security need not depend on Japan's participating in the game of nuclear deterrence.[20] Nevertheless, those who now anticipate a serious Chinese nuclear threat may foreshadow a public reaction that is not now manifest only because an active Chinese nuclear posture has not yet materialized. Official statements suggest that Japan's nuclear abstention is contingent upon a confidence in the credibility of America's nuclear deterrent, which it no longer automatically takes for granted.[21]

[20] Speech to Foreign Correspondents' Club of Japan, Tokyo, March 5, 1970.

[21] For example, Foreign Minister Aiichi stated in 1969, "It is not thought that China's present nuclear weapons are weapons which can be deployed as a threat toward Japan. We do not feel such a threat as their attacking us tomorrow. This is because Japan is taking a setup [sic] for defending its security. If this setup is removed, it is not known as to whether they will pose a threat or not" (*Sankei*, March 21, 1969).

JAPAN'S VIEW OF AMERICA'S SECURITY ROLE

Since 1947 the Japanese government has consistently pursued a policy of committing the United States to protect Japan by means of a mutual defense arrangement—a military alliance—designed to counter the communist threat to the homeland and South Korea.[22] Calculating that the United States shares this security interest, Japanese leaders have sought to build and consolidate a mutual defense arrangement on the basis of a U.S. guarantee, the deployment of U.S. forces in areas adjacent to Japan, and U.S. use of bases in Japan. Within this arrangement they have tried to retain as much autonomous control over Japan's internal defense and American use of its bases as Japanese capabilities and American deference would permit.

With the passage of time the internal threat has subsided, and Japan has gained exclusive control of its internal security. In order to protect the homeland from external as well as internal attack, Japan, initially in response to American urgings, has rearmed. Now America's role in insular defense is confined principally to nuclear deterrence and naval protection. But for regional security Japan is as dependent as ever on the United States.

Japan first formally recognized that its security depends on American protection of South Korea

[22] This theme is traced and examined in Martin E. Weinstein, *Japan's Postwar Defense Policy, 1947–1968* (New York: Columbia University Press, 1971), beginning with the memorandum prepared by Foreign Minister Ashida and handed to the U.S. government on September 10, 1947 (pp. 24–25).

when Prime Minister Yoshida and Secretary of State Acheson, upon signing the Security Treaty in September, 1951, exchanged notes supporting this objective by military cooperation with the United States. The independence of South Korea remains Japan's most immediate and compelling security interest outside insular and Okinawan defense, just as keeping Korea out of hostile hands was the keystone of Japanese imperial policy before World War II. From the beginning of its mutual security agreements with the United States, however, the Japanese government has successfully resisted occasional efforts by American officials, most strenuously exerted by Ambassador John Foster Dulles during the Korean war, to induce Japan to commit its own forces to South Korea or any other country. Instead, Japanese leaders have regarded America's regional security role as the necessary condition for Japan's adherence to purely insular defense, thereby avoiding a role that would jeopardize Japan's internal cohesion and its good relations with Asian nations.

Thus, for compelling internal and external political reasons as well as for national security, Japan has pursued a policy of keeping the United States credibly committed to the defense of South Korea and adjacent areas as well as to the defense of the home islands. It has regarded the stationing of American forces in Japan and Okinawa and the establishment of bases for American military operations in the area not only as necessary measures of collaboration to satisfy Japanese security requirements but also as the means of keeping American power engaged in the area and of eliciting closer consultation with the United States on matters of mutual security interest. Gradually the Japanese government has succeeded in reducing the American presence in Japan and gaining autonomous control over America's use of military facilities, recognizing that progress toward this end is the political condition for keeping America's engagement acceptable to the Japanese public. But just as the culmination of the process—the agreement to the reversion of Okinawa—has been achieved, the government has come to realize that the major political obstacle to keeping the United States engaged may lie less in Japanese nationalism than in American congressional and public pressure for retrenchment.

The prospect of American disengagement from East Asia threatens the foundation of Japan's postwar security policy and brings to the forefront the politically painful and potentially divisive issues, hitherto suppressed when the nation could be more confident of American protection, concerning the scope of Japan's security interests and military policies beyond self-defense. The way Japan and the United States respond to this new situation will have a critical effect on Japan's role in Asia.

On the surface and for the time being the Japanese reaction to American retrenchment is moderate and exerts no impact on Japan's security policies. The Nixon Doctrine, the Mansfield Resolution, reductions of general purpose forces, press accounts of the opposition of American youth and other dissenters to American involvement in Asia, Henry Kissinger's and President Nixon's trips to China, the imposition of an American surtax aimed at Japanese exports, and various signs of a shift toward "neo-isolationism" have created an undertone of uncertainty and apprehension about the reliability of Japan's security bargain with the United States. Yet the American decision to withdraw 20,000 men from South Korea was generally welcomed in the Japanese mass media by military affairs analysts and by political spokesmen of opposition parties. Government officials, although somewhat surprised at the scale of America's decision, maintained, in accordance with America's official explanation, that the reduction of American forces was based on the most careful assessment of the military balance and that the remaining American forces were adequate to uphold the U.S. commitment, considering the growth of South Korean military strength. The equanimity with which they responded to the news of American withdrawals is partly a reflection of their low estimate of the threat of communist aggression; but this estimate is attributed, in part, to the American presence.

Reductions of the American military presence in the Philippines and Taiwan occasioned no concern in government circles. Scarcely any note was taken of them in the press; and this commentary was entirely favorable, since the reductions were viewed as a contribution to the reduction of tensions between the United States and the People's Republic of China.

The withdrawal of American air squadrons from Japan received a good deal of press commentary, but the few muted expressions of concern about the scale and timing of the withdrawal were insignificant when weighed against the widespread confidence in the minimal nature of the Chinese and Soviet threat and against national satisfaction with the removal of the last vestiges of the American occupation.

Even when one asks Japanese analysts of political and military affairs what their response would be to the complete withdrawal of American forces from the adjacent area, including abandonment of the use of bases in Japan, many will insist that this would not affect Japanese security enough to necessitate a change in Japan's defense policy unless the Chinese or Soviet threat were to increase dramatically. Some are strengthened in this conviction by the dubious assumption that the United States could support the same security objectives well enough from Pacific bases, but the principal ground for their view is confidence that Japan's insular security will withstand any threat short of a communist occupation of South Korea or Taiwan.

It would be a mistake, however, to conclude from this evidence that Japan will calmly accommodate itself to such a significant change in the foundation of its postwar policy as the Nixon Doctrine signifies. Informal conversations with journalists and academics who follow Japanese opinion confirm other signs of official Japanese concern about American retrenchment. They indicate that America's pursuit of a lower posture in Asia will be anything but serene in the long run, unless Japan should be favored by the happy combination of a high degree of peace and harmony in its international environment and an extraordinarily sensitive and reassuring diplomacy on the part of the United States.

As in the case of the European allies' approach to American troops in Germany, the Japanese are less concerned with the technical adequacy of American armed forces than with the American will to use them. Therefore, the size and deployment of American forces is less significant per se than when and how the United States seems likely to use them and where they seem to fit into the total context of America's relations with Japan and other Asian states.

Observing the overall shift in the direction of American foreign policy—manifested as clearly in official justifications, congressional and public sentiment for retrenchment, and budgetary stringencies as in force reduction—few Japanese who follow foreign affairs closely can escape the impression that the credibility, if not the capability, of American forces to protect the area near Japan is significantly declining. Nongovernmental observers express this view quite freely. They seriously doubt that the United States would intervene with its forces to protect South Korea unless the North Koreans launched a massive invasion and American troops were stationed in the South.

Japanese officials revealed similar doubts and apprehensions about the American will to uphold its commitments when they expressed their concern prior to the admission of the People's Republic of China to the United Nations that expulsion of Taiwan from the United Nations would encourage Americans to wash their hands of the obligation to protect the Republic of China. Widespread recognition of Peking as the sole government of China, they argued, would soon follow, and with it, the loss of American will to defend Taiwan by intervening in what would then be viewed as a civil war. Similarly, official reaffirmations of America's defense commitment to Taiwan and of America's bonds with Japan, in connection with President Nixon's journey to China, did not overcome persistent suspicions in Japan of some secret deal between Washington and Peking to arrange spheres of influence against Tokyo's interests.

Naturally, such doubts about the credibility of American power and commitments in Asia are accentuated by American efforts to normalize diplomatic relations with China, especially while Peking is vociferously decrying U.S. "collusion" in the rise of Japanese "militarism"—a position that Peking obviously stresses in its effort to divide the United States and Japan and settle the Taiwan issue before the United States, it fears, turns Taiwan over to Japan. Moreover, given these doubts, any worsening of Japanese-American relations even on matters not directly related to American security obligations and military policies (for example, trade relations) tends to undermine confidence in the reliability of American security guarantees.

In this respect, the Japanese are particularly sensitive to diplomatic procedures which imply that the United States assigns a higher priority to accommodations with China than to close relations with its ally. The hurt shock in the Japanese government attending Washington's failure to consult or even inform it about Henry Kissinger's mission to Peking and President Nixon's decision to follow, is an obvious case in point. It reminds one of the similar problem the United States has encountered in relations with its European allies, but the problem in Asia is more difficult to manage because America's relations with Japan are not sustained by anything like the network of historical, cultural, and personal ties that the United States has with Europe, nor by the institutional and procedural lines of communication and collaboration. The Japanese, moreover, are quite sensitive to this difference and believe that it reflects America's substantially lower evaluation of its interests in Asia as compared to Europe. The president's pledge to keep American troops in Europe indefinitely in the face of domestic pressures for substantial withdrawals and the enforcement of cutbacks elsewhere is a tangible confirmation, in Japanese eyes, of a substantive priority of interests that portends America's declining will to involve itself in Asia as the vestiges of the cold war fade.

Nevertheless, the declining credibility of American power in Asia, as the Japanese see it now, does not require any change in Japanese defense policy. Indeed, the overt manifestations of Japanese apprehension about American retrenchment are reserved for expressions of keen dismay about the resulting expectation that Japan will begin to take over the American role—and for staunch denials that this will ever happen. This stance, however, reflects more than Japanese concern about the fears and charges of resurgent Japanese militarism that are rising in other nations. It is an implicit recognition that the logic of a devolution of power from the United States to Japan may some day find significant proponents in Japan itself.

American retrenchment also exerts important indirect effects on Japan's foreign and military policies. It affects the fears and expectations of other states with respect to Japan's position in Asia, and Japan's policies respond to these fears and expectations. The most conspicuous and immediate indirect effect of American retrenchment results from the apprehensions of other states that Japan will undertake a regional military role and become a nuclear power. These apprehensions reinforce Japan's determination to limit its military role in order to reassure others of its pacific, nonmilitary policy. On the other hand, what would happen to this self-constraint if the United States could no longer be relied upon to provide military protection to its Asian allies? In that case might not some Asian states who are now opposed to a Japanese regional military role find military assistance and even a military guarantee from Japan acceptable if this seemed necessary to offset Chinese or Soviet influence?

Charges of resurgent Japanese militarism are most vocal in communist countries. Peking and Moscow charge not only that Japan aspires to become an aggressive military power with nuclear weapons but also that the United States, in order to share its defense burden in accordance with the Nixon Doctrine, is supporting Japan's ambition by turning over to it a large part of America's military responsibilities, possibly within a new regional bloc of reactionary states under Japanese leadership. As evidence of Japan's new imperialistic role they point with particular alarm to the rapid growth of the Self-Defense Forces.

One might suppose that communist states would be especially frightened by the prospect of Japan striking out on its own, free from the constraints and assurances of its alliance with the United States, but in fact they remain dedicated to the primary objective of isolating Japan from the United States. Their public alarms are still directed against the Security Treaty as much as against the transfer of power to Japan within it, since the danger they proclaim is America's exploitation of Japanese militarism to advance its own imperialist designs at a lower level of direct involvement.[23] Peking, moreover, has a special reason for wanting to split Japan from the United States: an isolated Japan, in its view, is less likely to take over America's protection of Taiwan.

Within the present framework of policy Japan feels no pressure to restrict its defense program further because of communist fears and propaganda, but communist charges do tend to reinforce the exist-

[23] In his interview with Chou En-lai on August 9, 1971, James Reston invited Chou to explain his desire to see the U.S.-Japanese security pact broken in view of the likelihood that this would impel Japan to go nuclear. Chou replied that this treaty does not prevent but actually assists Japan's resurgence as a military power and that Japan's military expansion will inevitably follow its economic expansion overseas. He cited fifty years of suffering at Japan's hands and referred to signs of the beginning of Japanese militarism. In conclusion he observed, "When you oppose a danger, you should oppose it when it is only budding." But if Japan should give up its "ambitions of aggression against Korea and China's Taiwan," he added, "then it will be possible for China and Japan to conclude a mutual nonaggression treaty on the basis of the five principles of peaceful coexistence" (*New York Times,* August 10, 1971, p. 14).

ing constraints on Japan's military role. The fear of
provoking displays of Chinese hostility is particularly constraining, since China, as its imposition of
political conditions on trade with Japanese com-
panies implies, has some leverage on Japanese policy,
and since the Japanese entertain undaunted hopes
and expectations of harmonious relations with China.
On the other hand, if Japan should some day decide
to become an active "pole" in a multipolar Asian
balance of power (whether out of insecurity or ambition or both), the evident importance that Peking
and Moscow ascribe to Japan's military potential
could become a formidable diplomatic lever in the
hands of a prudent and clever Japanese government.

In contrast to the communist states, most noncommunist states in Asia are ambivalent, though
apprehensive, about the expansion of Japan's military forces and their role. On the one hand, the
noncommunist countries fear a Japanese regional
military role because it might lead to a revival of
Japanese militarism and dominance. Indonesia, with
visions of its own preponderance in Southeast Asia,
and South Korea, with its long history of Japanese
domination, are particularly opposed to this hypothetical development. Throughout Southeast Asia
apprehension about the possible military ascendance
of Japan is aggravated by antipathy to Japan's growing economic preponderance in the area. Moreover,
the prospect of a Japanese regional military role
is regarded as quite likely in the next decade, among
the few Southeast Asians who have begun to think
about such things. The overseas extension of Japan's
military power, it is thought, will come about as the
result of the expansion of Japan's economic interests

in Asia, increasing competition for trade and influence between Japan and China, and, above all, the decline of America's power in the area.

On the other hand, Japan's Asian neighbors seem less categorically opposed to a Japanese overseas military role than the Japanese assume. From the rather pragmatic attitudes they take toward this possibility now one might reasonably infer that within the next five to ten years many of the noncommunist countries in Asia might accept, and some (for example, Taiwan) might even welcome, Japanese military assistance in some form if they thought it was needed as a counterpoise to China in order to compensate for the declining American presence. Weapons and equipment or an expanded naval role would be the most acceptable forms of Japanese assistance. Military assistance and guarantees in the context of a multinational Asian organization or a U.N.-sponsored group would be more palatable than bilateral Japanese aid.

The equanimity with which Asians might greet such a shift in Japan's military role would vary in direct proportion to their confidence in a residual American security role and the strength of the American alliance with Japan. For, notwithstanding familiar complaints about the overbearing American presence, Asian governments in recent years have been markedly anxious that America's own reaction against overcommitment should not lead to a complete or precipitate disengagement from the area. They have been anxious not only because they want the stabilizing influence of a counterpoise to communist states—and the United States, alone among the possible counterpoises, is recognized as having no imperial interests in Asia—but also because they value the constraints of the American alliance upon Japan. For these reasons leaders in Taiwan and South Korea have made a particular point of urging the United States not to undertake any drastic or hasty disengagement. For the same reasons an independent Japanese nuclear force would be extremely disturbing to Asian states, since, even though it were regarded as a counter to China's nuclear force, it would signify that Japan had ceased to rely on the American guarantee.

IX. JAPAN'S DEFENSE POLICY

Japan's defense policy has faithfully mirrored the prevailing consensus about Japanese security interests, the requirements of Article 9 and of domestic cohesion, the low estimate of external threats, and reliance on effective American support of American commitments in the Far East. The general effect has been to restrict the armed forces to a size, armament, and mission appropriate only to insular defense. Nonetheless, this policy has produced a sizable military establishment, which casts a political shadow far larger than its limited mission.

The defense budget for 1971 (about $1.2 billion) was more than four times the budget for 1954. This increase reflected the transformation of an internal police force into a modern military establishment designed to cope with external as well as internal attacks on the homeland. The initial draft of the Fourth Defense Plan for fiscal years 1972 through 1976 aimed to strengthen Japan's defense capabilities still further. It doubled military expenditures in the Third Defense Plan to the level of $16 billion (¥5.8 billion) over five years and moved up Japan's annual defense spending from twelfth to seventh in the world. It projected an annual increase in defense expenditures of 18.8 percent.

Domestic and foreign criticism of this scale of military spending led defenders of the budget to reemphasize its defensive nature and its modest size compared to the total national budget, total expenditures, and GNP. In behalf of this contention it could be pointed out that since 1960 Japan's defense budgets have been less than 10 percent and a declining proportion of the total government budget, and that they have been 1 percent or less of the GNP.[24] Defense expenditures have been running at about 50 percent of expenditures on education and social welfare. These proportions are officially cited as a matter of national policy and are regarded as the statistical expression of the basis for continued widespread public support of Japan's defense program.

[24] As a basis of comparison with other states the Japan Defense Agency's so-called White Paper listed a number of ratios of national defense expenditures to GNP, based on 1970 figures for the former and 1969 figures for the latter, taken from the Institute for Strategic Studies' annual report on the world military balance. Among these are: United States, 8.6 percent; Soviet Union, 8.3 percent; People's Republic of China, 9 percent; United Kingdom, 5.1 percent; Australia, 4 percent; Sweden, 4 percent; Israel, 25.1 percent; United Arab Republic, 13.3 percent; North Korea, 24.9 percent; South Korea, 9.2 percent.

Another basis for public support lies in the fact that defense spending has been concentrated on technology rather than on manpower. Thus the target for ground forces (a target not yet reached in 1971) is fixed at 180,000. This figure reflects, in part, the difficulty of recruiting volunteers in a period of full civilian employment, but it also reflects the policy of keeping forces down to a level that cannot impinge on the civilian sector of public life or be used to undertake foreign operations.

In its White Paper of 1970 the Japan Defense Agency reiterated in some detail the constitutional and political limits upon the weapons and missions of the Self-Defense Forces (SDF). Defense Minister Nakasone went out of his way to renounce nuclear weapons and an overseas conventional military role. Using a favorite figure of speech to make his point, he described Japan's defense posture as "the combination of a rabbit with long ears and a porcupine plus the Security Treaty with the U.S." In October, 1971, Nakasone's successor for a short period, Naomi Nishimura, went even farther in explicitly renouncing an expansion of Japan's military role:

In other words, our self-defense capability is the last resort reserved for the survival of our nation. As stipulated in Article 9 of our Constitution, we will never resort to armed means in settling international conflicts.

This principle will be applied to the protection of our overseas economic interests and assets. I would like to make it very clear that we will not use our self-defense capability even for such a purpose. In my view, the use of military means to protect overseas interests is not only anachronistic but useless. Protection must and can be provided, in the era of negotiation, first by diplomatic persuasion and second, if that fails and interests are violated, by economic measures such as compensations to the victims. I can assure you that no self-defense force unit or personnel will be sent overseas to protect Japan's economic interests by force.[25]

In spite of these various explicit and implicit limitations upon Japan's defense program, however, the SDF is a rather formidable "porcupine" in its particular environment, and it is a porcupine whose continued growth is bound to make neighbors uneasy. If the initial draft of the Fourth Defense Plan were carried out, the SDF would contain, in addition to 180,000 ground troops, 990 tanks, 200 ships (principally destroyers and submarines) totaling 247,000 tons, 920 aircraft (including 180 F104J Starfighter and over 158 F4 EJ Phantom interceptors), and NIKE-AJAX surface-to-air missiles. This force, critics pointed out, would include jet fighters with a range greater than the B-24 bombers of World War II and capable of carrying nuclear bombs, two 8000-ton DDH six-helicopter carriers for anti-

[25] Speech at Foreign Correspondents' Club, Tokyo, on October 11, 1971. Significantly, however, Nishimura added, "I must hasten to add, though, that such a comprehensive security concept is neither practical nor feasible if Japan fails to gain the cooperation of other countries. In particular such a limited security effort has not so far created any major fear among our people mainly because of the existence of Japan's security relationship with the U.S."

submarine warfare (which became a special object of parliamentary and interservice controversy), and 240 new and larger tanks (which are difficult to justify except on grounds of prestige and symbolic value). Its defensive mission, moreover, has been extended to cover a wide zone of air and sea interception surrounding the broad area of the home islands, which now encompass Okinawa. In theory, Nakasone said, the Constitution does not prohibit SDF forces from operating hundreds of miles away from the main islands in order to protect the merchant fleet or, he might have added, to prevent intrusion into Japanese air space by hostile aircraft.[26] Some Japanese analysts believe that neither the spirit of the Constitution nor domestic opinion need prevent Japan from participating with the United States in air and sea operations in Korean or Formosan waters. They would draw the line only at the use of Japanese troops abroad or Japan's engagement in a political/military commitment in behalf of these countries.

The ambiguity of the distinction between self-defense and the defense of surrounding areas is compounded by the tendency of the U.S. government, particularly officials of the Department of Defense, to merge the two, if only by failing to make the distinction explicit when urging the Japanese government to increase its contribution to collective defense and praising increases in its defense program. The resulting implication—not entirely without foundation—that Americans want to transfer the general burden of area defense to Japan as the

[26] Interview with foreign correspondents on March 5, 1970.

United States reduces its presence accentuates Japanese apprehension about the size and composition of the SDF and aggravates domestic political contention over the defense budget.

Understandably, therefore, the anxious question has been asked in Japan and outside Japan: Where will the building of the SDF stop? For at the present rate of expenditure Japan might have one of the most powerful armed forces in the world in another ten or fifteen years. Regardless of the restrictions on its weapons and missions, an armed force of this magnitude might make a qualitative change in Japan's position in Asia. It could scarcely be regarded as a purely passive force, no more related to external policy than Switzerland's army.

Anticipating this possibility, Japanese leaders indicated in 1971 that some sort of ceiling would be placed on the expansion of the SDF. Only 80 percent of the envisaged size of the SDF, they said, would be attained by the end of the Fourth Defense Plan. Furthermore, in October, 1971, Defense Director Nishimura, citing the recession in Japan's economy and the "dollar shock," said he had decided to retrench the initial draft of the Fourth Defense Plan by 10 percent through reduction of the first-line combat weapons, deferring the purchase of a number of aircraft and other items. Nonetheless, in February, 1972, the government proposed and the Cabinet approved a budget for fiscal year 1972–73 increasing military spending by 19.7 percent to the equivalent of $2.6 billion. The increase, intended to compensate for the revaluation of the yen and the decline of the growth rate, resulted from the earmarking of funds for the first year of the five-year buildup, including $90 million for the production of 20 T-2 supersonic jet trainers; but the budget also included a sum for the procurement of F4 EJ Phantom aircraft. This budget, however, provoked such vigorous opposition that the Japanese Parliament was paralyzed for a record twenty days before a compromise was reached in a revised budget submitted in February, 1972, removing for the time being an appropriation for some new aircraft and freezing $294 billion earmarked for disbursement after the coming fiscal year, pending formal approval of the new buildup by the National Defense Council.

Whatever modifications of the Fourth Defense Plan or the annual defense budgets may be made in response to economic conditions or domestic opposition, it is evident that those who shape Japan's defense program regard all limits on the SDF as conditional, being particularly dependent on the status of America's military capabilities and will, communist behavior, and the requirements of maintaining domestic support for the military establishment. Japan's approach to nuclear weapons is no less pragmatic and conditional.[27] As we have noted, Japan's adherence to the "three nonnuclear principles" is regarded largely as a matter of policy, subject to change (particularly with respect to tactical or defensive nuclear weapons) if political and

[27] This subject is thoroughly examined in Shelton Williams, *Non-Proliferation in International Politics: The Japanese Case,* University of Denver Social Science Series in World Affairs (Denver, 1972). See also Victor Gilinsky and Paul Langer, *Japanese Civilian Nuclear Program* (RAND Corporation, RM-5366-PR, August, 1967).

military conditions should basically change. Japanese leaders, conscious that the government can produce nuclear weapons if it wants to, regard the nuclear option as a resource they hope Japan will not need to use. But just as nuclear abstention is a matter of choice, so nuclear acquisition would have to be the result of a conscious political decision.[28] Such a decision would have to be preceded by an open debate, which would go to the core of Japan's foreign policy and security interests.

The nuclear *option,* on the other hand, has been created not so much by open debate and decision as by the government's peaceful nuclear energy program. Although Japan's leaders were aware of the military implications of this program, the option results, in the first instance, from the great increase in Japan's plutonium production that will accompany the projected expansion of its nuclear energy facilities for the generation of electricity.[29] These facilities, together with the capacity of the governmental Power Reactor Corporation (established in 1967) to process plutonium for nuclear warheads and assemble

[28] In 1971 Ryukichi Imai, chief of the nuclear fuel section of the Japan Atomic Power Company and consultant to the International Atomic Energy Agency, attracted considerable attention among experts in government and private atomic energy enterprise with his "N minus 2" plan, which is designed to establish a number of technical and procedural safeguards against Japan attaining the ability to produce nuclear weapons without an open political decision, after which production would take two years. But in its detail and sophistication this plan was unique.

[29] Japan's Atomic Power Industry Council has estimated that atomic power stations will supply 16 percent of the national electricity demand in 1980 and almost 40 percent by 1990.

them, mean that Japan by the end of the 1970s will be able to produce enough nuclear warheads (say, one hundred a year) for a more-than-token nuclear force. The anticipated construction of enriched uranium reactors could add another fifty warheads a year capacity.

The Japanese nuclear energy program now depends on the importation of enriched uranium from the United States, but Japan's Long Range Atomic Energy Program of 1967 envisions the development of an "independent fuel cycle" that will greatly reduce Japan's dependence on imported fuel and reactors and fulfill the government's goal of making nuclear energy the main source of electrical energy. This program for achieving substantial independence in nuclear energy would surely be accelerated if the United States were to substantially raise the price of exported nuclear fuel or try to manipulate its export of fuel so as to affect Japan's nuclear weapons capacity or policy.

From the standpoint of estimating the prospect of Japan's becoming a nuclear power, however, it is not only important to know that Japan has the physical capacity to produce warheads within about two years of making such a decision. It is just as important to recognize that the utilization of nuclear energy for military purposes would require a conscious and conspicuous political decision supported by a number of specific and observable technical measures.

The situation is comparable with respect to the development of nuclear weapon delivery vehicles. Japan's rocketry program is an essentially civilian enterprise without government supervision or central

planning. Having advanced through four genera-
tions of rockets, it produced in the mid-1960s two
multistage missiles, the Lambda and the Mu. The
latter missile is similar to the first U.S. Minuteman
intercontinental missile. In February, 1970, Japanese
rocket experts moved another step toward a delivery
capability when they succeeded in launching a satel-
lite. But Japanese rocketry still lacks some indispensable elements of a nuclear delivery system. Most
important among these elements are the technology
for reentry and for guidance and control. Consequently, to convert the rocket program into an
IRBM program would probably take a crash effort
of three years. The development of reentry tech-
nique could scarcely be disguised as nonweapon research. And a military program would require re-
organization of the space program under centralized
government control.

Legal obstacles to the production of nuclear
weapons help assure that Japan's decision to go
nuclear would be open and deliberate. The Atomic
Energy Basic Law would have to be repealed. Even
the inspection provisions of the International Atomic
Energy Agency, which Japan has accepted for imported reactors and nuclear fuel, tend to deter nuclear production. Although technically the provisions
might be violated without detection, they are probably effective enough to make the decision to produce warheads open. Japan's ratification of the Non-
Proliferation Treaty, which it signed in 1970, would
have the same political effect, although inspection
provisions would probably be even less exacting and
the treaty can be abrogated upon only three months'

notice on the ground that "extraordinary events" have jeopardized the nation's "supreme interests."

The real obstacles to nuclear acquisition, however, are the popular war-born inhibitions against nuclear armament and the government's calculation of Japan's security needs. The first obstacle could become subordinate to the second if the international political basis of the prevailing consensus on Japan's defense and foreign policies should fundamentally change.

Already the quality of popular antipathy to nuclear armament has changed. With the fading of World War II memories and the erosion of the legacy of American occupation, with the resurgence of national pride and self-confidence and the impact of Prime Minister Sato's campaign to overcome the nation's "nuclear allergy," Japanese no longer approach the subject of nuclear armament as such an emotion-laden taboo. Now they view nuclear abstention more as a pragmatic policy responding to certain internal and external conditions, and they feel much freer to discuss the advantages and disadvantages of nuclear armament in public than two or three years ago. The accession to political power of a generation that does not remember Hiroshima and Nagasaki, let alone Manchuria and Pearl Harbor, will accentuate this change of attitude.

Only an insignificant number of Japanese publicly advocate nuclear armament for Japan. Public opinion polls indicate that only 20 percent favor Japan's acquisition of nuclear weapons. But the significant point is that the policy of nuclear abstention, once an axiomatic article of faith, has now become a matter of practical judgment.

Indicative of this approach is the extent to which Japanese opponents of nuclear armament inside and outside the government have recently emphasized the technical and physical obstacles to acquiring a useful nuclear force. Japan, they point out, is so small and densely populated that a retaliatory force could be disarmed by a first strike, and ABMs could not prevent civil obliteration against a determined attack. This is a persuasive argument, but it could yield to technical developments—for example, sea-based nuclear forces—and, conceivably, to the kind of psycho-political strategic arguments that French strategists and statesmen developed under de Gaulle's regime. If Japanese national pride were joined with sufficient fear of Chinese or Soviet hostility and American unreliability, Japan might decide to arm with nuclear weapons for purely defensive reasons.

If the conditions of Japanese security should change fundamentally, one need not presuppose a resurgence of right-wing nationalism to imagine the nation growing accustomed to the idea of "going nuclear." This process would probably begin with the step-by-step adoption of an overseas military policy—not a policy thrust upon unwilling neighbors but one cautiously instituted with their approval and even their explicit request, beginning with the sale of military equipment. The fact that such a transformation of Japanese policy would probably be taken deliberately and openly and accompanied by considerable debate would not prevent it from taking place piecemeal and gradually.

At present, undertaking an overseas military policy seems like such a huge departure that Japanese typically argue against it on all-or-nothing grounds. Since it is unthinkable that Japan should try to protect the full range of its external interests, sea-lanes and all, Japan ought to stick to purely insular defense, the argument goes. But one suspects that if the conditions of Japanese security seemed to change fundamentally, all the reasons that now constrain Japan from going beyond insular defense would persuade the government to shift gradually to an overseas military policy. One need not assume that this shift would lead inevitably to nuclear armament, for nuclear armament raises different issues and is impeded by quite special constraints. But the abandonment of pure self-defense would certainly remove an important psychological obstacle to nuclear acquisition. Japanese proponents of such a change would probably be as eager to depreciate the importance of the change, by assuring the nation and the world that the adoption of an overseas military policy would not lead to nuclear armament, as they are now wont to argue against such a policy on the grounds that one step down this path must lead the whole way. But the new position would be as fallible as the present one, for the reality of Japan's military posture tends to strain the limits of its underlying concepts and intentions.

X. THE INTERNATIONAL STRUCTURE OF POWER AND INTEREST

Before turning to the implications for U.S.-Japanese relations of the foregoing analysis of factors shaping Japan's position in Asia, we should consider the international configuration of power and interests within which these relations may develop. There are too many possible patterns of international conflict and alignment in the next decade or two to make it worthwhile considering each one. Reasoned conjecture cannot go much farther than extrapolating from currently perceptible facts and trends.

Observers of the Asian scene generally agree that we are now witnessing the erosion or at least complication of the familiar stable structure of relationships in Asia and the development of a quadrilateral balance of power among the United States, the Soviet Union, China, and Japan. This balance is a product of countervailing political and diplomatic maneuvers for stakes short of territorial-political control. It has not yet consolidated into a stable pattern. With the exception of Soviet mobilization on China's northern border, the stakes are not *directly* related to military power, although military considerations (such as the credibility of America's supporting its commitments and the magnitude and scope of Japan's military policy) play a significant role in the background. Thus we appear to be entering one of those periods of history in which fluid maneuvers for political influence and status predominate, while military confrontations and the formation of military coalitions seem a rather remote possibility. At the same time, the maneuverers are so constrained by the prospect of countervailing maneuvers and by the very fluidity and uncertainty of the patterns of conflict and alignment that they play with considerable circumspection and caution.

Eventually, historical examples lead one to expect, the patterns of international conflict and alignment will consolidate. Then, perhaps, the international politics of Asia will begin to resemble the politics of confrontation, coalition, and deterrence that prevailed in the familiar cold war, but in a multipolar rather than a bipolar configuration. Meanwhile, one can imagine many different patterns of relationships within an incipient quadrilateral balance, but at present there appear to be two relatively stable relationships—U.S.-Japanese alliance and Sino-Soviet hostility—with several overlapping configurations of shifting diplomatic conflicts and alignments:

a) *A tripolar Sino-Soviet-American balance.* Each state seeks to keep the other two from concerting their policies and political moves. Chinese and American policies occasionally converge for particular ends, including the deterrence of Soviet military action against China and the fostering of constraints on Soviet power in Eastern Europe and South Asia. From the American standpoint this relationship is oriented primarily toward non-Asian stakes: to make the Soviet Union more tractable and less dangerous, particularly in Europe and the Middle East. For China it is oriented toward security against the Soviet Union and toward global competition for influence in the less developed countries. Limited leverage on Moscow is inherent in this tripolar configuration of power and interests, but to be effective from the American standpoint it must be used with a delicate hand and publicly disavowed, partly to preserve flexibility in relations with China and partly to keep open the global lines of negotiation and accommodation with the Soviet Union. In this tripolar relationship the Soviets are largely on the defensive, as they see it, although their defensive actions are hostile and dangerous from the Chinese standpoint. The apparent Soviet approach to the brink of a surgical strike against Chinese nuclear facilities in 1969 and the deployment of 600,000 battle-ready troops along the Chinese border may manifest the Soviets' almost pathological fear of China as a dedicated heretical communist rival, but Peking has viewed these actions as threats to China's very survival and has consequently hastened its overture to Washington. The Soviet Union's alliance with India, its long-standing protectorate over Outer Mongolia, its competition with China for influence in Pyongyang and Hanoi, and its overtures to noncommunist states in Southeast Asia are part of Moscow's effort to contain China; but they look like encirclement to Peking.

b) *A more recently emerging tripolar balance involving the United States, Japan, and China.* In this relationship China, moved by deep and seemingly ineradicable fear of Japan, seeks to contain the resurgence of Japan in Asia. It also seeks to remove the American presence from Asia. Although it must increasingly confront a potential conflict between these two goals, for the time being Peking concentrates upon splitting the U.S.-Japanese alliance, playing off one member against the other, aiming to prevent the United States from assisting Japan's resurgence, and, more specifically, to impede the United States from transferring the protection of Taiwan to Japan. Peking can be expected to move alternately closer to the United States or to Japan, depending on the opportunities to alienate the one from the other, but China's hostile reaction to Japan's growing economic preponderance in South Korea, Taiwan, and Southeast Asia will lead it to concentrate increasingly upon fostering fears of Japanese militarism. The United States and Japan, on the other hand, have more limited interests in this tripolar relationship. They seek to limit China's ambitions and influence and to normalize relations with her while guarding against either ally getting so close to China as to disadvantage the other. But neither the United States nor Japan basically seeks an advantage against the other; rather each seeks closer relations with China in order to pacify the People's Republic and gain leverage in relations with the Soviet Union.[30]

c) *A less developed but probably increasingly important Sino-Soviet-Japanese balance.* The People's Republic of China views economic relations with Japan primarily as an instrument of leverage on Japanese domestic politics and foreign policy. The Soviet Union views them as an instrument for the

[30] Although many Japanese and some Americans look longingly at the prospect of great trade opportunities developing with populous China, these opportunities are in fact quite limited unless China should decide to reverse its policy of pursuing autarky. See Alexander Eckstein, *Communist China's Economic Growth and Trade* (New York: McGraw-Hill, 1966); Dwight H. Perkins, "Is There a China Market?" *Foreign Policy,* Winter, 1971–72, pp. 88–106.

development of Siberia and the alignment of Japan against China. Japan will naturally try to exploit the Sino-Soviet rivalry in order to restrain both communist powers and gain special national objectives in the area, such as the recovery of the Northern Islands. Yet Japan cannot move too far toward one rival without sacrificing something in its relations with the other. To fulfill its potential role in the quadrilateral balance, this relationship awaits a clearer Soviet initiative to come to terms with Japan on Siberian economic development.[31] American-Chinese rapprochement may provide the political opportunity and incentive for promoting such an initiative.

In this structure of relationships the United States has considerable room for maneuvering as compared to any of the other states. It has no deep conflicts of interest with China as long as the Taiwan issue can be kept quiescent. It has economic differences with Japan but basically the same security interests against China and the Soviet Union. The Soviet

[31] In seven years of Russo-Japanese talks about Siberian development, only two agreements for Siberian lumber and pulp in exchange for machinery and consumer goods have been signed, in addition to separately negotiated trade agreements. The talks have revealed that mutual economic incentives alone are not sufficient to lead to important agreements for the cooperative development of Siberia, and that only the mutual perception of substantial political advantages can overcome existing internal and external political constraints. The history of the incentives and constraints affecting talks on the joint development of Siberia is cogently analyzed by David I. Hitchcock, Jr., "Joint Development of Siberia: A Study of Decision-making in Japanese-Soviet Relations" (unpublished paper, The School of Advanced International Studies, Johns Hopkins University, May, 1970).

Union and China, on the other hand, are firmly locked into formidable constraints of mutual hostility; while China's deep fear of Japan imposes strict limits on Sino-Japanese rapprochement, and Japan's antipathy to the Soviets and the limits to what the Soviets can offer Japan similarly limit Soviet-Japanese cooperation.

Japan, too, might find considerable leverage in this developing configuration of power and interests if it wanted to play one state off against the other in an adventurous diplomacy, but in reality it is constrained by its lingering dependence on the United States and by its internally and externally imposed inhibitions against a bold foreign and military policy. If Japan were less constrained, Asian politics would be more fluid and tense (particularly Sino-Japanese relations), but after a possibly dangerous period of adjustment to Japan's new role, there might emerge a reasonably stable tripolar Sino-Soviet-Japanese balance that would constrain the major states in Asia with only peripheral American involvement.

Given this multipolar configuration of power among the major Asian states, the smaller states of Southeast Asia, while looking increasingly to Japan for economic but not yet military assistance, seem inclined to seek, separately or in rudimentary coalition, to diversify their links to the major powers in order not to become too dependent on any of them. Their ideal may be to seek guarantees from the major states of their security and neutrality. The ideal would be facilitated if they could implement it as a group; for example, in ASEAN. But it remains to be seen whether current diversities of interest and of relationships with the major states will yield to the logic of regional coalition.

Not the least advantage of the more pluralistic and delineated configuration of interests and power that seems to be developing in East Asia would be the normalization of China's foreign relations on a more traditional state-to-state basis, as Peking felt compelled to make the kinds of nonideological strategic and tactical compromises that have increasingly complicated Moscow's diplomacy. Not that the People's Republic of China would abandon its revolutionary goals or even its revolutionary instruments of policy. Indeed, it will probably look upon its new role on the central stage of world politics as an opportunity to reach new mass audiences in Japan, the United States, and other developed countries with its political messages. But given a fairly stable balance of power in Asia, Peking's more active participation in a growing range of state-to-state relations is bound to lead China to subordinate revolutionary goals and tactics to the imperatives of power and influence in a complex pattern of international politics. In this environment there is reason to expect not only that China will be effectively contained but also that China will contain others.

In a relatively fluid multipolar balance of power, particular events or crises, internally or externally, may alter and consolidate the pattern of conflict and alignment into a more structured relationship. Foremost among the external loci of such events or crises is the Korean peninsula, since there the interests of all the four major states converge; and there the prospect of any change in the American or Japanese roles is bound to exert an immediate political effect.[32] Already the official visits to China have touched off a reassessment of foreign relations in North and South Korea. South Korea is worried about the withdrawal of American troops and the reliability of its American ally. North Korea professes to see the prospect of withdrawal, coupled with American acceptance of China's "five principles of coexistence" in the Shanghai communique of February 27, 1972, as an opportunity to move toward the peaceful unification or federation of the two Koreas on acceptable terms. The Sino-American rapprochement and the prospect of American withdrawal also raise new fears in both Koreas of a larger Japanese role in South Korea. South Korean fears may be qualified, as time goes on, by recognition that Japan's large stake in Korea might be used to salvage South Korean security. North Korean fears may spark a genuine search for an internationally agreed *modus vivendi* on the peninsula.

The prospect of a larger Japanese role in Korea also worries Peking and, to some extent, Moscow. At the same time, neither Peking nor Moscow would view its rival's filling the vacuum of influence left by American withdrawal with any more equanimity than it would view Japan in that role. Therefore, in the absence of a settlement that would stabilize the relationship of the two Koreas to the satisfaction

---

[32] Changing factors in the relationship of the two Koreas to each other and in the relationship of the four major states to the two Koreas and one another are examined in Morton Abramowitz, *Moving the Glacier: The Two Koreas and the Powers,* Adelphia Papers, no. 80 (International Institute for Strategic Studies, August, 1971).

of the major powers, any basic erosion of American protection of South Korea is bound to be unsettling. But because this prospect is unsettling it may also help consolidate and stabilize the quadrilateral pattern of international relationships in East Asia. The United States cannot control this process of consolidation, but it can affect it more than any other state. For the maintenance or withdrawal of its forces in South Korea and the general context of policy within which it disposes these forces will be a catalyst of changing U.S.-Japanese relations, which in turn will shape the whole structure of Asian relationships.

XI. U.S.-JAPANESE SECURITY RELATIONSHIPS

We have noted that Japan's dependence on America's conventional and nuclear power within the framework of the Security Treaty is the keystone of its foreign policy; but that the prospect of American disengagement now calls into question the reliability of the keystone, which in turn compels the Japanese to face awkward questions about their nation's military role. In this circumstance the present U.S.-Japanese relationship is in danger of eroding. It may nevertheless be the best feasible relationship, but three alternatives deserve to be considered, if only to highlight the problems of maintaining present policies:

1. U.S. military disengagement, with Japan ad-

hering to the existing geographical and political constraints on its military policy.

2. U.S. disengagement, accompanied by the devolution from the United States to Japan of some security responsibilities beyond the defense of the homeland.

3. Continuing U.S. engagement, accompanied by closer terms of military collaboration—constituting an integral U.S.-Japanese partnership—with the United States bearing exclusive responsibility for the security of Japan's international environment beyond Japan itself.

The first alternative, leading either to a disarmed or armed, possibly nuclear, isolation of Japan, would logically be accompanied by active accommodation of potential adversaries and deemphasis of alliance with the United States in favor of a more neutral stance. This might well be the strategy Japan would try to pursue if American political and military disengagement from East Asia should seem inevitable. But one must conclude from the foregoing analysis that a purely insular defense policy under the conditions of American disengagement would not last for long unless Chinese and Soviet behavior should seem so beneficent—toward Japan and toward South Korea and Taiwan—as to enable the Japanese to feel virtually as secure as now. This is possible but unlikely. Not only is Japan, unlike Switzerland or Sweden, too important for other states to leave alone, but without credible American protection even the acquisition of a nuclear force would not be likely to relieve Japan of the sense that its security required some projection of Japanese conventional military power beyond present limits in order to contain the extension of Chinese and Russian power and guard against hostile actions in Northeast Asia. The hiatus left by the withdrawal of the United States from South Korea would be most immediately threatening, since, according to the historic pattern of relationships, each of Korea's big neighbors (Japan, Russia, and China) would be inclined to counter the threat of any of the others supplanting the American position by securing a paramount position for itself. It is unlikely that Japan would stay out of this tripolar game at the risk of ceding paramountcy to either of the other two players.

As an alternative to the geographical and political extension of its military power Japan might rely on Soviet friendship and support, sweetened perhaps by the reversion to Japan of some Northern Islands in return for Japanese aid in the development of Siberia. This arrangement presupposes a considerably more forthcoming Soviet attitude than heretofore, but American disengagement and Sino-American rapprochement might provide the political conditions for such a change. A Soviet-Japanese entente, combined with the crystallization of Sino-Japanese accommodation based on Japan's acceptance of the People's Republic as the sole representative of China and its renunciation of any security arrangements with South Korea, would be a logical response to American disengagement. But here the logic of *Realpolitik* must contend with the psychology of national feelings, which cast doubt upon the supposition that the Japanese government would regard any arrangement with the Soviet Union as a sufficient substitute for the American presence or an adequate alternative to the expansion of its own power.

Therefore, Japan's isolation, whether armed or unarmed, would tend to lead to a more heavily armed and geographically extended involvement. With its ties to the United States loosened or severed, Japan's pursuit of this role would accentuate Sino-Japanese tensions and destabilize the Korean equilibrium. These developments would, in turn, increase Japan's sense of insecurity and tend to drive her toward the kind of militant posture that her neighbors fear. If this is the likely result of American disengagement combined with Japanese isolation, it can be argued that the United States should pursue an orderly and concerted devolution of power to Japan rather than let it come by default as the result of frustration and insecurity.

The second alternative—a controlled transfer of power and responsibilities from the United States to Japan—conforms to historic principles of *Realpolitik*, but we have seen that there are formidable political obstacles to Japan's carrying it out and some troublesome consequences to consider if Japan were to succeed. Therefore, the third alternative is likely to look increasingly attractive. After examining this alternative we shall be in a better position to consider the second.

Ironically, Japan's substantial achievement of "autonomy" in self-defense (along with the other side of autonomy, the reduction of America's presence and authority) has in some respects made American political and physical engagement in East Asia more valuable. In Japanese and in some foreign eyes the perpetuation of America's security role within the alliance serves as reassurance against the fears that Japanese "autonomy" will lead to Japanese "militarism." "Militarism" is an emotionally loaded term that could signify anything from an active diplomatic role backed by military power in support of overseas objectives to a resurgence of offensive right-wing nationalism sustained by a Guallist nuclear posture. One may reasonably challenge the relevance of this word, given the domestic and international constraints under which Japan now operates; but historical memories linger, and the apprehension and distrust they kindle in many nations, including the United States, are realities of political life. Consequently, to allay fears of militarism some Japanese leaders have recently emphasized the limits of Japan's autonomy. For example, they have reiterated the view that autonomous defense does not mean "single-handed" defense. This implicit recognition of the enhanced value of American engagement, however, leaves open the question of what terms of engagement are feasible if the United States is to remain the exclusive protector of mutual security interests outside Japan. On what terms of collaboration with Japan can the United States be expected to remain convincingly engaged, yet tactfully detached?

If America's European strategy is analogous, the way to stabilize American engagement in behalf of mutual security interests is the way it has been done in NATO: through close military collaboration in plans and operations and burden sharing in order to enlarge the scope of allied participation, while leaving the United States exclusive responsibility for the control of nuclear weapons and the preponderant role in managing the military balance. As applied to Japan, this formula would leave the United States with exclusive responsibility for the security of Japan's external environment in return for greater Japanese participation in joint security affairs. In this way Americans could be shown that Japan is a willing collaborator carrying an appropriate share of military responsibilities and burdens. And Japanese, on the other hand, could be shown that America respects Japan's autonomy and treats Japan as an equal partner. On this basis the United States and Japan might develop a network of institutionalized and informal communications and procedures which would give both nations practical incentives to elaborate their entanglement on a basis of mutual respect. Viewed in the perspective of this kind of relationship, the agreement for the reversion of Okinawa would be a step not toward disengagement but toward stabilizing America's engagement on terms of collaboration adapted to the political and technical requirements of the future.

This view pervades the report (released on December 28, 1970) of the Study Committee on National Security Problems, a private committee of eminent Japanese defense and foreign policy experts, which recommended the consolidation and reduction of U.S. bases on Okinawa and the Japanese mainland. One of its principal conclusions is that:

> The end of permanent stationing of U.S. troops presupposes a shift to a co-operative strategy based on the mobility of U.S. forces and re-entry of the bases in case of emergency. Japanese-U.S. consultative machinery should be established to

effect coordination of strategy for "co-operation in case of emergency."

The Committee recognized, however, that:

"Co-operation in case of emergency" will not work when political relations are strained. In the future, it will become necessary for the two countries to institutionalize a ministerial-level conference on foreign and national defense policies and to make continuing efforts through this machinery for the adjustment of the interests of both countries.

Clearly, this extent of Japanese-American co-operation presupposes a very close correspondence of security interests and of foreign policies as well. It puts a premium on candid, trusting, and tactful working relations. Japanese deference or acquiescence to American policies and actions in the period of American tutelage is no test of the prospects of harmonious relations under conditions of integral partnership. One must wonder, therefore, whether the United States and Japan have a sufficient convergence of external interests or even a sufficient political and cultural basis for understanding each other to create and sustain anything like the intimate relationship the United States and its European allies enjoy.

One critical test of the quality of cooperation between the United States and Japan will be whether they can reach reliable arrangements for the use of Okinawa and other Japanese bases in order to provide American air support and, if necessary, American troops to assist the Republic of South Korea to resist aggression. Considering that American use of these bases is now contingent on Japanese consent after consultation, reliable arrangements must depend upon close collaboration in military operations and contingency planning. It remains to be seen whether Japanese and American conceptions of security and foreign policy with respect to Korea are sufficiently close to provide the political basis for this kind of collaboration. What is in question is not so much the availability of Japanese bases to U.S. forces in the event of a massive, clearly unprovoked North Korean invasion but, rather, the correspondence of the views of the Japanese and American governments in marginal cases; for example, American deterrent deployments in response to a massing of North Korean forces on the South Korean border, or American air support in the event of border warfare growing out of an ambiguous mixture of diplomatic conflict, military raids, insurgency, and counteractions.

Of course, the decision to act (which means enabling the United States to act) or not act in defense of South Korea and other Asian states would have to be made as each situation arises and is judged on its merits. But in the absence of agreed guidelines and operating procedures comparable to the detailed consensus underlying military cooperation between the United States and its European allies, ad hoc improvisation may not be good enough to keep the United States engaged, the South Koreans secure, and the North Koreans deterred. In one sense, this is an argument for an integral partnership; but if the political basis for such a partnership is lacking, it argues for a looser not a tighter association.

The rationale of sustaining America's engagement through an integral partnership, however, lies not only in restraining Japan and maintaining the security of the area. It lies also in undergirding stable, moderated international relationships and, more specifically, in pacifying and defusing trouble spots that might otherwise undermine Japanese security and drive Japan toward a full military posture.

Korea will be the most dangerous trouble spot as long as the mainland Chinese are unwilling and unable to invade Taiwan. Maintaining American forces in South Korea may be the price of stabilizing the peninsula and avoiding a situation that would seem to pose a choice between South Korean insecurity, Chinese or Soviet paramountcy, or Japan's assumption of America's security role.[33] In this case, U.S. engagement in South Korea can be regarded as the linchpin of an integral partnership, and the close working relationship of an integral partnership, in turn, as the condition for keeping American forces engaged. On the other hand, if American forces are likely to be withdrawn sooner or later, it may be prudent now to start working toward some political substitute for American protection while American troops remain. In this case, defusing the Korean peninsula will also require the engagement of American forces in South Korea, but primarily

[33] This thesis is expounded by Pyong-Choon Hahm, Special Assistant to the President of Korea, in "Korea and the Emerging Asian Power Balance," *Foreign Affairs*, 50 (January, 1972): 339–50.

as an instrument for achieving a political substitute through a Korean *modus vivendi*. Achieving a *modus vivendi*, in turn, would require intimate consultation and cooperation between Washington and Tokyo.

Here an analogy to the prevailing strategy of European détente may be relevant. The strategy would be to bring about through a series of negotiations among the United States, the Soviet Union, China, and possibly Japan, and also between the two Koreas, an internationally agreed *modus vivendi* between North and South Korea on a basis something like the German formula of two states within a single nation.[34] This arrangement might be secured by arms control provisions and supplemented by agreements on trade and on exchanges of technology and personnel. It would be facilitated by using the withdrawal of American troops in South Korea as a bargaining lever, just as American troops in Europe are ostensibly to be reduced as part of an East-West "mutual balanced force reduction."

Barring some such Korean détente, it can be argued that the unilateral withdrawal of American troops would undermine the very conditions of Japanese security and constraint that an integral partnership is supposed to maintain. The only thing worse than unilateral withdrawal, according to this view, would be to permit the security of South Korea to erode while American troops were still stationed in the country, for then the United States would incur the worst features of engagement and disengagement.

[34] The application of the German analogy to a Korean accommodation is outlined in Abramowitz, *Moving the Glacier*.

This possibility of falling between two stools in Korea is the most critical specific case of a general disadvantage of integral partnership: By tying the United States into close military and political engagement, integral partnership would incur at least the added political burden, if not the military risk, of America's retaining responsibility for the security of Japan's international environment without being able to satisfy the Japanese that U.S. protection is adequate. This burden is likely to increase as China deploys a nuclear force. Indeed, the problem of preserving Japanese confidence and cooperation could become so burdensome that U.S. relations with Japan would deteriorate more seriously than if Japan were responsible for its own regional security. For the United States would add to the liabilities of inadequate reassurance to the Japanese the onus for Japan's military impotence. The Japanese, in their confusion and frustration, would naturally tend to blame their problems increasingly on the inadequacy of American guardianship rather than on their own indecision. Espousal of the general objectives of nuclear nonproliferation and Asian international order could scarcely relieve the United States from the political burden of impeding greater Japanese military self-reliance—a burden that Japanese leaders would be happy to shift from their own shoulders. In Japan's dependent status the slightest sign of an American entente with Peking, the slightest gesture of détente that was not checked out with Tokyo in advance, could strain the partnership, and Chinese or Soviet overtures to Japan might accentuate parallel suspicions of collusion in the United States.

In a period of history in which Japanese and American foreign policies seem destined to become increasingly differentiated, U.S.-Japanese relations as a whole are not likely to allay such suspicions.

Under these conditions, it is doubtful that Japan would play the beneficent role of a demilitarized political and economic power promoting the stability of Asia in harmonious partnership with the United States. More likely, Japan would be pulled in two conflicting directions: armed neutrality and isolation, on the one hand, or militant nationalism, on the other. The net result would be a kind of chronic internal crisis and external paralysis. As for the United States, increasingly irritated by Japanese criticism and lack of cooperation, it would be sorely tempted to seek refuge from the burdens of unrequited partnership through political disengagement. But an American disengagement that took place because of frustration, antagonism, drift, and default would not be nearly as conducive to a reasonably stable and satisfactory new structure of international relationships in Asia as disengagement that took place by design.

Of course, none of these strains and hazards of trying to sustain close cooperation with Japan need materialize or become unmanageable, but it would be imprudent for the American government to overlook the possibility before investing its dwindling political and military capital in the difficult venture of achieving an integral partnership with Japan. So rather than simply let its present position erode while Japan becomes an increasingly insecure economic giant locked into false isolation by its military impotence, the United States, it can be argued, should seriously consider investing its capital in the promise of a genuine but limited and orderly transfer of power to its resurgent ally. Needless to say, however, the desirability and feasibility of a real devolution of power can no more be taken for granted than the status quo, unilateral disengagement, or the achievement of integral partnership.

XII. DEVOLUTION OF POWER

The case for a devolution of military power and obligations from the United States to Japan rests, first of all, on the premise that the United States has important security interests in Asia and, second, on the supposition that these interests should and could be supported at a substantially lower level of American effort and involvement if Japan were to extend its military power and responsibility in their behalf. The case is also based on the premise that the United States can help induce Japan to shift its military role in this direction.

The objective of devolution would be not merely to relieve the United States of material burdens. Equally important, devolution would be intended to relieve the United States of the political and psychological burden of bearing such exclusive and direct responsibility as in the past for maintaining an international environment congenial to the mutual security interests of the United States and Japan in Asia, and for maintaining Japan's satisfaction and cooperation in the pursuit of this end.

On these grounds the devolution of power has a strong appeal to Americans. But it also evokes the image of a recapitulation of Japanese behavior in the 1930s and 1940s, which frightens and repels Americans and everyone else, including most Japanese. This image, moreover, now merges with the specter of a nuclear Japan and of the nuclear contagion spreading to other "nuclear threshold" states. The fear of Japan going nuclear is one of the dominant motives behind America's policy of retaining exclusive responsibility for Japan's security outside the homeland.

In reality, fears of Japanese military expansion and nuclear adventurism are overblown. The Japanese have had their military expansionism; they are not going to repeat it. The domestic and external constraints against any such course are prohibitively high now. The implied analogy to the world before World War II is misleading. Nuclear inhibitions, moreover, add a great deal to the constraints against territorial expansion or the search for hegemony. And there is no reason to think that Japan is more likely to use nuclear weapons provocatively or dangerously than, say, France. If Japanese acquisition of nuclear weapons should make more likely the spread of nuclear capabilities, the possibly adverse consequences still ought to be assessed in terms of the full consequences of devolution, including possibly beneficial ones, rather than simply dismissed in the abstract as a threat to world order. Among the possible benefits of a Japanese nuclear force, the United States should consider the political burden it may otherwise incur in maintaining the credibility of its nuclear umbrella in East Asia when China deploys a more impressive nuclear force.

In any case, whatever the consequences of a Japanese nuclear force may be, it is not self-evident that expansion of Japan's conventional military role would lead inexorably to nuclear armament. As we have indicated, there are some special, formidable obstacles to nuclear acquisition that do not impede the expansion of the role of nonnuclear weapons. And Japan may reap some of the advantages of nuclear *armament* while avoiding the liabilities, simply by perfecting its nuclear *potential*.

Moreover, it would be a mistake to think of devolution only in terms of a sudden, total transfer of American military functions in East Asia. A politically feasible program of devolution would envisage Japan acquiring no more than limited new security responsibilities confined at the outset to South Korea and Taiwan and the surrounding seas. It would envisage these responsibilities being acquired gradually in cooperation with the United States while the potential military and political hostility posed by China and the Soviet Union remained at a low level. Implicit in such a vision, too, is the assumption that America's interests in containing communist expansion in Asia are at least no greater and probably less than Japan's. Thus the most favorable model of devolution, as distinct from the model envisioned in familiar discourse on this question, does not require a sudden total transfer of power within the past framework of containment; rather it envisions a gradual limited transfer of power within the framework of a downward revision of American interests and a declining communist threat to those interests.

Nor could devolution realistically presuppose the emergence in the next decade of new regional organizations to supplant America's previous military role. Among other obstacles to any such radical change in the structure of Asian relationships, the nations of Asia lack sufficient convergence of political interests and sufficient perception of common security needs. Instead, the anticipated structure of power would be essentially a further development of the present incipient quadrilateral balance, in which diplomatic and political moves, exercised in behalf of limited political stakes, would be the primary levers of power and of countervailing restraints upon power, while armed forces would loom passively in the wings or, as in the case of Soviet deployments on China's borders, lurk menacingly at the entrances of the diplomatic stage.

But here we come to a more substantial argument against devolution. Would not the emergence of Japan as an overseas military power, like the United States and the Soviet Union, disturb the present pluralistic pattern of diplomatic maneuver by injecting into this system of moderated international conflict and alignment those abrasive concerns about military defense, deterrence, and the balance of power that pervaded the cold war before confrontation gave way to détente? If the present system of international relations in Asia permits American retrenchment without disengagement, why go to all the trouble of seeking the transfer of military tasks from the United States to Japan? If to some extent Japan's military potential, even though not fully developed or applied, lends weight to its participation in the present international system, what could be gained by a Japanese military role beyond defense of the homeland?

Basically, the hypothetical advantage of devolution is that it might enhance Japan's political leverage and reduce America's responsibility for the consequences in a period of increasingly active diplomatic maneuver in which the United States will otherwise be saddled with political and military burdens greater than it now anticipates. According to this view, the orderly transfer of America's Northeast Asian military responsibilities to Japan would substantially relieve the United States of the political burdens of a declining hegemony—a hegemony that perpetuates American responsibility for Japanese security under conditions of increasingly divergent interests in a field of diplomatic maneuver over which the United States will have decreasing control in any case. Regardless of American engagement, it can be argued, the present period of maneuver is bound to run its course as political alignments and conflicts become more clearly defined. Then Japan's attainment of a military posture more nearly commensurate with its interests and with the power of the other participants in the Asian balance might provide the basis for a stable, more structured configuration of power and interests. This configuration would be essentially a tripolar Sino-Soviet-Japanese balance, which would permit the United States to be a peripheral rather than a major power in Asia.

Against this hypothetical advantage of devolution, one must weigh the general disadvantage of America's relative loss of control over the diplo-

matic field of play, coupled with the uncertain stability of the new balance, in which Japan's active
role might raise the level of tension and confrontation. But if the scope of America's vital interests in
Asia is as limited as any realistic plan of devolution
must assume, the United States might regard the
loss of direct control and the risk of a more volatile
balance as a price well worth paying for the accom-
panying reduction of direct involvement.

After all, America's vital interest in Asia has long
since ceased to be the Open Door in China. Nor is
it any longer conceived to be tantamount to the
protection of all Asian nations from communist
aggression. It is now, in the prevailing American
outlook, practically confined to the preservation of
a secure and friendly Japan. The vitality of the
U.S.-Japanese alliance is essential to this end, but
its vitality may now depend on a larger measure of
Japanese self-reliance than can ever emerge as long
as Japan's military responsibility is confined to
self-defense.

If, under the conditions of an increasingly fluid
international pattern of conflict and alignment, the
United States were to pretend that Japan's security interests were more important to it than to
Japan, Japanese-American relations might become
so strained by mutual frustrations and resentments
as to destroy mutual confidence in the alliance and
leave Japan isolated in the face of blandishments
or intimidations by China and the Soviet Union. The
result of any such erosion of alliance would not be
consoling to those who fear a Japanese nuclear
force. Whereas Japan's assumption of a larger
military role might well be a step toward nuclear

acquisition, the erosion of Japanese-American co-hesion under the present constraints on Japan's role would be even more likely to lead in that direction. A nuclear-armed Japan alienated from the United States would be far more disturbing than a nuclear-armed Japan still operating within the framework of mutual alignment and accommodation.

If this line of argument for a limited transfer of security responsibility from the United States to Japan makes sense as a goal—a somewhat subjective and incalculable point which I shall leave to the reader's judgment—it is nonetheless a goal that would be hard to carry out; perhaps prohibitively so. In addition to the domestic reasons why the Japanese would be reluctant to abandon the constraints of insular defense, there are formidable external obstacles.

For one thing, a Japanese overseas military role presupposes that other states will seek Japanese military assistance in one form or another, but this would require a transformation of policy and atti-tude on their part that is scarcely indicated by any current signs. If devolution were to take place gradu-ally with Japanese cooperation and not suddenly as a unilateral act—if it were to leave America's politi-cal engagement within the bounds of the Security Treaty intact—then conceivably, though it now seems quite improbable, a number of noncommunist Asian states might accept and even welcome Japan's new role, but only if they were sufficiently frightened by China. China, realizing this, is unlikely to pro-voke such fear.

It is even less likely that South Korea, the neigh-boring country whose security is regarded as the most important to Japan's security, would welcome Japanese protection. To be sure, some working collaboration between Japan and South Korea in air and sea defense has developed, but Americans have played the decisive role of middleman in making collaboration politically possible. So strong are historical Japanese-Korean antipathies that most Japanese believe the Koreans would rather fight them than see them supplant the Americans. More likely, South Korea, once convinced that the United States was pulling out, would try to reach some sort of protective accommodation with China and North Korea. This may be taken as an argument for defusing Korea as the condition for American disengagement, rather than as an argument against devolution. But considering the difficulties of achieving a Korean *modus vivendi,* it would be risky to base devolution on the prospect of détente.

A Japanese overseas military role also presupposes that if Asian states should seek Japanese military assistance, Japan would grant it. If it is unlikely that Japan, in the event of a Korean conflict, would permit the United States to use bases in Japan in order to protect South Korea, except under the most unambiguous circumstances, it is even more unlikely that Japan would assume responsibilities that would directly involve it in a Korean war. Similarly, with respect to the Nationalist Chinese: Even assuming that the government on Taiwan might seek Japanese military support, it is doubtful that Japan would regard the political costs of worsened relations with Peking worth the purported advancement of the security of Taiwan.

III. THE LIMITS OF AMERICAN POWER AND INTERESTS

In choosing a policy direction, the U.S. government must be aware of the limits of its power and its interests. It is evident, for example, that American disengagement would not automatically lead to a devolution of power to Japan. At the same time, it is *not* evident that the United States could facilitate such a devolution by design. The United States simply may not have that kind of influence.

Japan's view of its security interests and of the advantages and disadvantages of undertaking a larger military role to support them will be the determining factor in the future of U.S.-Japanese relations. Japan will act only on the basis of a solid consensus on this vital issue. The American government can exert very little effective influence on this consensus by *direct* means. America's greatest lever of *indirect* influence is the control of its military presence and commitments in the area. But the United States would be ill-advised to use this lever in behalf of any policy that departed significantly from the Japanese consensus.

The worst thing that could happen to relations between Japan and the United States, and to their relations with other states, would be for the United States to press Japan to assume a larger military role when the Japanese were opposed to this course. Next worse would be for the United States to press Japan not to expand its military role if the Japanese were inclined to do so. For there is no American interest in Asia that does not depend on America's

91

central interest in maintaining the vitality of its alliance with Japan; and one prerequisite of its vitality, given the passing of American tutelage, is that the Japanese be allowed to make up their own minds on their role in Asia and to do so in response to changing external conditions rather than in response to American advice or pressure.

But the U.S. government should make up its mind, too. Is it prepared to pay the price of continuing American engagement in Asia in order to underwrite a system of multipolar diplomatic maneuver and to discourage Japan from playing a full-scale military role? Or is it willing to incur the risks and costs of disengagement for the possible advantages (but dubious feasibility) of facilitating an orderly devolution of power to Japan? Do Americans want a full-scale Sino-Soviet-Japanese balance of power in Asia while the United States withdraws to a peripheral role? Or do they prefer to preserve the vestiges of American tutelage over Japan in order to retain a major role in the Asian balance of power?

In reality, questions like these are seldom posed or answered in terms of such simple dichotomies, so far as policymakers are concerned. In the absence of any guarantee of a more promising alternative, American policymakers will prefer to maintain the present division of security responsibilities between the United States and Japan as long as they can while hoping that the constraints of an increasingly pluralistic pattern of diplomacy in Asia will compensate for the declining American military presence and the growing divergence of American and Japanese policies within the loosening bonds of the alliance. Such pragmatism may indeed be the wisest course to pursue in a transitional period that is full of uncertainties, but one hopes that it will be pursued out of a deliberate assessment of the pitfalls as well as the advantages. One hopes that pragmatism will be enlightened by careful consideration of the analytical alternatives rather than followed simply because it looks like the line of least resistance.

America's relations with Japan will be the cumulative product of incremental responses to the flow of specific issues that happen to come before the U.S. government for some sort of decision to act or not to act. But implicit in such responses will be certain broad judgments about American "interests" —an ambiguous word which I take to stand for the value attributed to international situations that one might reasonably want to see come about or not come about. This is the most basic yet obscure question of all facing the United States. What are America's really important interests in Asia? What are the interests, if any, for which Americans are willing to pay the political, economic, and possibly military costs of involvement with Japan?

Even in Europe this question is difficult to answer in terms of the conventional standard of American "security," because by this standard (if we mean only the territorial and political protection of the United States from foreign attack) there is scarcely any situation one can reasonably imagine occurring in any part of the world that would directly threaten us. On this narrow ground a policy of American isolation and nonintervention in Asia makes sense. On the other hand, if one defines the really important interests by such a generalized formula as a modicum of international order or a "structure of peace"—that is, an equilibrium among countervailing major-power pressures and influences entailing a minimal risk of armed conflict—there is scarcely any degree of American involvement that cannot be justified, save for political and economic constraints in the United States.

In Europe the question of American interest is less ambiguous because Americans have generally reached a firm judgment about the unique value of distinctive political and cultural affinities, consolidated by personal and institutional ties and associations. For this reason the security of Europe has attained such a high priority, even if the means of preserving it is in dispute, that Americans virtually identify it with the security of the United States. It remains to be seen whether the security of Japan will approach this same status. Ultimately, this is as much a question of the relation of national societies and cultures as of the governments of states to one another.

For half of this century America's Far Eastern policy suffered from the traumas and contradictions of a sentimental attachment to China and the Open Door which exceeded the actual willingness of the nation to exert its power in behalf of its proclaimed interests. This was followed by a period after the communist victory on the mainland of exaggerated disillusionment and fear in which America's image of the Chinese threat exceeded the real magnitude of China's power and intentions. With the moderation of U.S.-Chinese relations and the emergence of a powerful Japan no longer under American tutelage, a new era of American Far Eastern policy has begun. If the guidelines of American interest in this era are cloudier than before, one can nonetheless find compensation in the fact that they are likely to develop in a less emotional climate of opinion.

Library of Congress Cataloging in Publication Data

Osgood, Robert Endicott.
  The weary and the wary.

  (Studies in international affairs, no. 16)

  Includes bibliographical references.
  1. United States—Foreign relations—Japan.
  2. Japan—Foreign relations—United States.
  I. Title. II. Series: Washington Center of Foreign
  Policy Research. Studies in international affairs,
  no. 16.

E183.8.J3O83   327.73'052   71–186510
ISBN 0–8018–1393–X
ISBN 0–8018–1398–O   pbk.)